Resurr
From Death to Life

My Journey to God

Robin A. Wages

Mullen Press Publishing

www.MullenPress.com

Mullen Press Publishing
808 Gleneagles Ct #42301
Towson, MD 21284
www.mullenpress.com
contact.us@mullenpress.com

Publisher's Note: The information in this book is true and complete to the best of the author's knowledge. Any advice or recommendations are made without guarantee on the part of the author or publisher. The author and publisher disclaim any liability in connection with the use of this information.

Resurrection: From Death to Life/ Robin A. Wages. -- 1st ed.
Paperback ISBN 978-1-954016-15-6
Ebook ISBN 978-1-954016-16-3

Acknowledgment

Thank you, Jesus, for all you've done for me. I owe you my life, and I will spend the rest of it serving you with all my heart, mind, and strength. I would also like to thank my family, who sacrificed the most by letting me go to become everything God intended. I know there were days you wanted me home, but God had a different plan. I love you all. Finally, I thank the rest of you who pushed me closer to my destiny. I've learned so much on this journey and couldn't have gotten this far without you. I learned who I am in Christ because of you. Some relationships were good, and some bad. Some were long-term, and others were short-lived. However, all of them were important. In most cases, it did not feel good as I was going through it, but it all worked out for my good. The olive only became valuable when pressed, which caused the oil to be produced. I, too, through the process of being pressed, caused the anointing (oil) to be produced. This oil will now be used for the salvation, deliverance, and healing of God's people.

God Bless,

Robin Wages

Forward

When I first began writing this book, the words began to flow as a river or stream flows into the ocean. Halfway through, I realized that I spent more time talking about my issues than how God delivered me from those issues. Now, don't get me wrong, I believe it's important that you understand all that I went through because only then can you understand the significance of what God did. However, I want you to see all that happened so the message I am trying to convey comes through clearly. This book is my journey to God. My defeats and my wins, the ups and, yes, down. I feel the need to add this disclaimer. This book will be an accurate, transparent account of my life. It is meant to touch the heart of anyone reading it. I thought hard about what to put in it but soon realized I needed to be honest with myself and the people that would be reading it. How will you know how far God has brought me if I don't paint an accurate picture? I was jacked up and, based on the things I experienced, made horrible decisions at times. However, through it all, God still had a plan for me. This is my journey.

Foundational Scripture: John 11:21-26

21 "Lord," Martha said to Jesus, "if you had been here, my
brother would not have died. 22 But I know that even now
God will give you whatever you ask." 23 Jesus said to her,
"Your brother will rise again." 24 Martha answered, "I know
he will rise again in the resurrection at the last day." 25 Jesus
said to her, "I am the resurrection and the life. The one who
believes in me will live, even though they die; 26 and
whoever lives by believing in me will never die.

Using this scripture as a basis for my change, I will show you a series of events that unfolded in my life that eventually led to my deliverance. Some tests I passed, some I failed, but all of them are making me into the woman God intended. No, not because I said so, but because God said so. This was the path that He chose for me and not one that I would choose for myself. In fact, this was a journey I didn't want but was one I desperately needed. The only problem was I just didn't know it. However, if Jesus raised Lazarus from the dead, and He raised me, surely He can raise you. It doesn't matter how long you have been in the situation. It doesn't matter how bad the situation is. God and God alone can raise you back to life. Lazarus was physically dead. However, many of us are spiritually dead. I call to you now boldly, come forth in the name of Jesus.

It's Not the End (A Poem)

It's not the end, but the beginning
Satan, you tried to take everything I had
You tried to use the hurt and pain to make me bad
I serve notice on you today
God chose me as His vessel, and I'll follow His way
The race is not given to the swift or the strong
It's given to the one who continues to hold on
So, know I walk by faith and not by sight
Know that my God has given me the right
See, this wasn't the end God planned for me
But the beginning He orchestrated in making me free
So, thank you, God, for the ups and even downs
Thanks to you, I'm no longer bound
Like the woman my past says I used to be
Whatever lies there is now dead and, in the sea
So, as I look with my head held high
I know my God is looking from the sky
From the throne room, He watches me
Knowing on this day, I am truly free!

The End

Robin A. Wages 1/29/2017

Dedication

I dedicate this book to Jesus, my Savior and Lord. It is through Your unwavering love for me that I have made it this far on my journey. It is also through that same love I've learned to embrace life, the good, the bad, and the ugly, knowing that it all will work out for my good as long as I keep you first. I understand that without you, there would be no book and, in all honesty, no me. I was tired and desired to be with you. However, through this journey, you showed me another way by facing my demons, which led to my healing and deliverance. Thank You for becoming everything I needed, and I know I am forever grateful!

Before I formed thee in the belly I knew thee; and before thou camest forth out of the womb I sanctified thee, and I ordained thee a prophet unto the nations.

Jeremiah 1:5 KJV

Contents

CHAPTER ONE

The 1st Hour: Through the Eyes of a Child

"Wow, it's raining again today," I remembered thinking as I turned over in the bed. I could hear the booming of the lighting and the roaring of the thunder. "Hmm… Sounds like God is angry!"

However, I loved listening to the rain as it hit the top of the roof. I used to hate thunderstorms, but I now seem to enjoy them. I remember the old people used to say, "Stop moving around and be still and let the Lord work."

I guess that's what I did every time one came. I pulled the cover over my head and went back to sleep. However, today was different. I had a dream about a little girl who faced many challenges but refused to give up. She was a cute brown-skinned little girl with two shoulder-length ponytails. She was dressed in a pair of faded blue jeans with holes in the knee, a white shirt, and worn blue Converse tennis shoes. She seemed to be around six years old, which would have made it about 1975. She seemed tall for her age. However, the thing that stood out the most was her smile, or should I say the lack of it. She stood on the porch of what appeared to be a green and white house that her grandmother lived in, looking around with tears in her eyes. I could see three mailboxes that sat at the front of the property by the dirt road. There was a mobile home to the left as you pulled in, which was white and black, where her uncle fixed cars. There was also her aunt's mobile home, which was yellow and white and set slightly behind her grandmother's house. Finally, there was another uncle's mobile home, which was white and set directly behind the green and white house. It seemed to look raggedy and abandoned. The grass was high, and it had a horrible smell that came from it. I silently wondered what it all meant.

Then suddenly, I heard the Lord say, "Wake up and tell her story."

I dragged myself out of bed and stood before the mirror, thinking, "Lord, I'm in my 30s, newly divorced, broken, fat, and with many health issues. My life is jacked up, and I honestly can't understand why You would choose me to write this child's story. How could I possibly tell her story when my own life was a mess?" My pity party was interrupted by a loud boom. Jesus, I screamed as the thunder startled me. No need to be afraid that I'm in this alone now. I remember thinking, "Boy, the storm seems to have gotten worse." I sat down at my laptop, and instantly, I was in her body.

I began to see images of this little girl's life as God allowed me to see. However, I could barely get my thoughts together with all the noise going on outside. It became hard to focus; it seemed the more I tried to type, the worse the storm got. I prayed and asked God to give me the words.

He said, "I will give you the words by allowing you to see it all through her eyes. You both will become one because only then can you tell her story accurately."

As I began to type, I instantly became one with her in her body; I saw and felt everything she did. However, I struggled because her emotions were raw. She was filled with rage, insecurity, hurt, and pain. She felt unwanted and unloved, and I was experiencing it all firsthand. Here is her story.

***

The first memory I see is where she is sitting in her mother's chair, watching her smoke a cigarette. Suddenly, her mom blew smoke out of her mouth in the form of a circle. It floated towards the little girl. As it approached the little girl, she reached up and placed her finger on it, and the smoke seemed to stop in mid-air. As long as her finger remained on the smoke, it seemed suspended in time. However, when her arm grew tired, she pulled away, and the smoke vanished.

She thought, "What just happened?"

That day, she knew something was different about her. She just had no idea how different.

As the years passed, she noticed that something just didn't seem right. She wasn't a part of a loving family who took care of each other, at least not to her. In this family, they seem to thrive on hurting each other with words and sometimes even physical abuse. Something in her knew that this wasn't right. What she was feeling wasn't based on anything she had seen or heard. No, it was something deep within her. It appeared everything that went on in her family was normal. At least it was normal to them. However, she felt emotionally starved and unloved. Don't get me wrong, she knew her family loved her; after all, they were blood. She simply longed for something greater. To her, something was missing, as she didn't see acts of love or warmth. Their motto, it seemed, was to "Get it yourself or you won't eat."

So, looking through the eyes of this child's life seemed harsh and unbearable. She felt as if she didn't fit into the family that she was born into. It wasn't as if she didn't try to; however, she had compassion in a family that seemed compassionless. It was like wearing a coat that didn't seem to fit right. She simply did not fit in, and she struggled with that, it seemed, every day of her young life.

As I watched through her eyes, I really didn't see her growing up but rather surviving. I fought not to be overtaken by raw emotions and the desire to give up. Her story had to be told. She needed a voice in a world that didn't hear children. Deep within me, I begged that God would allow this cup to be passed from me. Jesus didn't respond. I guess everyone has a story to tell, and God had chosen me to tell hers. I wrote on.

Through her eyes, I could tell that she loved her family and that they loved her. However, she didn't understand that hurt people hurt people. She didn't understand that they loved her the only way they knew how. My heart broke for her! Can you imagine as a child not understanding why you don't fit into your own family? Why was your voice never heard, and why there were always feelings of not being good enough? All of this translated to "THEY DON'T CARE ABOUT ME!" Her pain is real, and this is her truth.

***

I paused, took a deep breath, and tried to pull myself together as the tears streamed down my face because I was experiencing her pain firsthand. Her anger, frustration, abandonment, and rejection seem to overtake me. I felt as though I could barely breathe because of the intensity of her emotions. The bottom line is that she was mad as hell, and I was experiencing all her raw emotions at one time. Startled, I heard the crack of the lightning and the roaring of the thunder; the storm was worsening.

I remember thinking, "WOW, it's really storming!"

As I came back to myself, I remember thinking, "I need to prepare for the storm because the lights are probably going to go out."

Not to mention, a girl has to eat, right? Besides, I also needed to check the batteries for the flashlight and radio and make sure my cell has a good charge. I needed to charge the charger as well.

"Lord, you know it's just you and me," I thought to myself.

God, you gave me wisdom, so I must walk in it, seeing how there's no man around to help me. Lord knows I do want one, but Lord, make him a good one.

My goodness, I have never seen a storm get so bad so fast. Oh well, I am as ready as I can be. The lights are starting to flicker, so I don't think I can type anymore tonight. Besides, the storm is so loud it scares me, and the truth is I can barely think. As I lay across the bed, waiting to fall asleep, I whispered this prayer:

Lord, you never told me who this little girl was, but please protect her tonight, Jesus. The storm is so bad, and I pray that she is okay. I pray that she is safe not just from the storm but from anything she may be going through. Hold her in your arms and let her know you are there even in what seems like the roughest of times. Amen

My mind began to wonder, "Is she still a child? If so, is she still alive? Had I ever met her before? Was she someone from the neighborhood? Who was this little girl?" There was something about her.

"Lord, there's something about her. I just can't put my finger on it," I said.

As I began to drift off to sleep, Jesus spoke and said, "Write!"

"God, can you at least tell me her name?"

He spoke softly, "Ann."

I sat on the side of the bed, wondering how I would ever be able to write with the storm going on outside.

God said, "Listen."

The storm had passed, and I hadn't noticed. I guess my mind was on Ann. I was really concerned about her. As I go to the computer to begin typing, I'm instantly back in her body.

***

This time, Ann was thinking about her grandmother. This brought tears to her eyes. She seemed to have no good memories that stood out. All she could feel was hurt and a sense of why? She didn't see her grandmother as a loving, positive role model. She wasn't nice to all grandchildren or even children from her point of view. Well, at least, not the females. Now, she would move heaven and earth for those boys. However, the girls were bitches, heifers, and hoes; at least Ann was. There were very few times Ann remembered being called anything endearing. Her grandmother's love was for hire with the girls.

You see, Ann's mom was a single parent and couldn't afford to give her grandmother as much as others could. No matter what her mom did, it was never good enough. Ann remembered hearing many conversations between them, or should I say arguments. They were always about the same thing, money.

"Why does the lack of money mean I'm not good enough to be loved?" Ann thought to herself.

I see Ann sitting in a room with tears running down her face. God allows me to overhear a conversation she is having within herself. Ann's mom, who was the second oldest, dropped out of school to help her parents around the house. She worked what jobs she could to take care of her own two children. None of that seemed to matter to old grandma. Grandma was a mean and hateful woman that everyone else seemed to love.

Ann's mind drifted to where vivid memories of pots or anything else her grandmother could get her hands on being thrown at her and other female cousins. What could warrant such behavior from an adult towards a child? I screamed in my own rage from the images that were being projected from this child's mind! Another image appeared of a day when one of her female cousins was sitting down with her legs open, playing. She had pants on, but their grandmother threatened to throw hot ashes in her ass. Yes, that's what she said.

I could see the tears welling up in Ann's eyes and then rolling down her cheek. Ann doesn't understand how someone that she was related to could be so mean and yet call it love. She was confused and frustrated; most of all, she was wounded, and she didn't even know it. Her grandmother was her first example of God's love and what the church was supposed to be about. She often heard her grandmother praying for a long time before bed at night and then experienced this hatefulness all day, Monday through Saturday. However, Sundays were different. They put on their Sunday best and headed off to church to learn about God. However, what she was seeing didn't line up with what she was hearing about this man named Jesus from the Pastor. What kind of God was this? She didn't even realize that these experiences would shape her relationship with God and with others for a very long time, and not necessarily in a good way.

Through the years, she learned to deal with the way things were. She didn't come around as much. In fact, she made herself scarce. She didn't remember things getting any better because her grandmother was always in someone's business. It was always drama, and when you got to the bottom of it, old grandma was the instigator. She affected the entire family in some way, shape, or form. Whether it was good or bad, she impacted them all. Ann believed in some way that her grandmother felt the girls had somehow stolen her youth as she aged and her health declined. In Ann's mind, dear old grandma was going to spend the rest of her days punishing them. Ann's emotions were high, and she felt this strongly. There could be no other answer in her mind! If she only understood that people aren't perfect and even though they confessed Jesus as their Savior, they still need Him as a deliverer because, in truth, we are all jacked up and in need of a Savior and deliverer.

***

Instantly, I'm back in my body. I took a deep breath, let out a sigh, and realized, "Oh, great, the storm is back."

I swear I've never lived or heard about a place that rained or stormed so much. However, my mind quickly moved back to Ann.

I whispered, "Lord, I pray she's okay. Heal her, Jesus, for her pain is real, deep, and overtaking her. She doesn't understand. God, she doesn't understand!"

I took a deep breath and wiped the tears from my eyes, pleading with God to help this little girl.

"Lord, how can I tell her story when I'm so concerned about her until I can't think? Lord, there needs to be an intervention; don't allow Ann to continue thinking her grandmother hated her. She probably loved her the only way she could. Lord, I wish I could talk to her and make her understand. God, you send me to so many others. Please send me to her. She is broken and bruised! God, she needs to know you love her, and even the people who hurt her love her; they simply don't know how to show it. She doesn't understand why you died or even who you died for. She is drawing conclusions about you from broken people who do not understand real love. My heart aches for her. This is too much to bear. Writing her story is breaking my heart. Why won't you let me go to her? She only wants to be loved. I can love her, God, just send me. Oh, God, just please send me!"

He does not speak.

My pleading with God is interrupted by the wind shaking the house. I decided to turn it in for the night. As I prepared for bed, I whispered, "Wow, the rain is really coming down."

I hear the rolling of the thunder and the cracking of the lightning. It seemed angry enough to kill. It's like it has feelings or something. This storm was too intense to be a regular storm. It felt more like a tornado or hurricane. However, there had been no mention of such a weather prediction when I watched the news earlier in the day.

"Hmm…That's strange. I don't remember them talking about even a light shower. That's odd," I thought. "Well, man is always trying to predict what God is going to do. I guess they got it wrong again. I wish I had someone to cuddle up with. I am really scared."

"God, you promised me a Godly husband. Well, he sure is taking his precious time…Good night, Jesus."

The lights went out, and the rain hitting the roof was the medicine I needed for my fear and weariness. As I slept, I began to dream about Ann. God showed me that I was becoming more comfortable in her body; I wasn't struggling as much anymore. It really bothered me that I couldn't see a clear view of her face to know who she was. I wondered if she was someone from the neighborhood that I could reach out to. I always saw her from within or watching a memory from behind. Her face is never visible to me.

God must've heard me talking in my spirit because He answered softly, "In time, you will know."

***

I woke up the next morning feeling refreshed, thinking that maybe everything that had happened was a dream. The storm was now a constant drizzle of rain. I honestly don't know why it rained so much in Columbia. Will the sun ever come out? It would be so nice to go for a walk in the sunshine. The Lord whispers, "Type!"

I guess it wasn't a dream after all. As I sat back at my desk, I slipped back into her body, realizing everything this little girl was going through would affect her life greatly for years and years to come. Poor thing would never know how much until it hits her head on through life and its challenges. I wanted to pray with her, but God said write. So, I started typing as the Spirit led.

***

Ann appeared to be around the age of 15 now. The ponytails were gone, and her thoughts went to the person who had given birth to her. She saw her mom as a very hard-hearted person. She had never seen her mom cry or sorrowfully emotional at any time that she could remember. She was one of the most strong-willed people Ann knew. Ann never heard her mother complain about anything. In fact, she went and did what she had to provide for Ann and her older sister. She appeared to be larger than life, Ms. Superwoman. She was the kind of person that if someone said she couldn't or wouldn't, she set out to prove them wrong.

Now, because her mom worked so much, Ann stayed with her uncle and aunt a lot. These seem to be pleasant times. There is no hurt or pain associated with these memories. She giggled as she remembered an incident that happened between her and her cousins. They placed a can on the stove to heat up some spaghetti, and it exploded all over the ceiling.

Ann yelled, "They are going to kill us!"

When her uncle and aunt came home, neither Ann nor her cousins said a word.

Her aunt saw the mess all over the ceiling, "Who did it?"

Everyone yelled in unison, "Not me!"

Ann's aunt said, "Well, I'm going to cut all yawl ass to make sure I got not me!"

Boy, they got the whooping of their lives. It's funny now, but it sure wasn't funny then. Ann had fond memories of being with her uncle and aunt because they traveled a lot, and Ann was always with them, so Ann got to go as well. Ann remembered places like Carowinds, Disney World, Maggie Valley, and Myrtle Beach. However, there were rare times that she was home with her mom.

Ann thought of the times her mom would be pulling water up out of the well and chopping wood. She remembered stacking wood. It's funny now because her mom made sure she knew how to cut, stack, and make a fire just in case the need should ever arise. She didn't want Ann to be dependent on a man or anyone. Ann's mom did tire and oil changes on her car. She cut the grass, raked the yard, and made all the repairs needed around the house. She did what she had to do to survive. Ann remembered one day, while playing in the yard, a big snake came across the porch. She started yelling, and her mom came to the door.

Ann yelled, "Don't open the door because there's a snake in front of it!"

Her mom never flinched. As soon as the snake passed by the door and dropped to the ground, she came out, took her hoe, and chopped the snake in two, killing it. Ann's mother picked the snake up and turned quickly to put it in the barrel to burn. It flew off the hoe and almost wrapped around her cousin's neck. Ann and her cousins were so scared, but oh, they did laugh once it was over. Ann's mom didn't' flinch. She was a rock. Her tough exterior just kind of went along with what Ann saw her do every day! She was Superwoman. Her mom was tough, no doubt; however, Ann felt that it affected her relationship with her mother. Ann didn't understand that her mom's hard exterior kept her going and had nothing to do with the love her mother had for her.

***

There was a thought that stuck out the most with this little girl. Ann was approximately eight years old, and this was the day she found out about her dad. She was told by her mother that her dad died in the war. Every now and then, Ann would ask her who he was. One day, she was fixing her bicycle on the porch when a man came down the street. Ann had seen him many times doing the same thing he was doing this particular day. He was jumping about three feet off the ground, cursing like you wouldn't believe, and drunk.

Ann had seen this man time and time again, but today, her mom looked up and nonchalantly said, "You've been asking me about your dad; well, there he is."

Ann stood and watched him for a few seconds, then stooped back down, deciding he was better off dead to her. Now Ann was told that she looked just like this man. They even said she had mannerisms like him. However, she felt she had no connection to him. It's strange because his parents lived three doors down from her, around the corner, and she had never known it before this day. As Ann got older, her mother wanted her to get to know her father and his side of the family. However, her dad still didn't want anything to do with her except when he was drunk.

Then he would come by screaming, "That's my damn daughter!"

Ann remembered her mom drawing back a hammer and swinging at him.

She told him, "Get away from her. If the only time you're going to come is when you are drunk, then don't come!"

As he walked away, Ann's mom said to her, "I will introduce you to his mother and father."

She did just that.

Shortly after, her mom said, "You're old enough to develop a relationship with them if you want one."

Ann soon realized she didn't want one. Ann remembered a conversation she overheard between her mother and her dad's mom. It seemed her mom was going off because Ann's grandmother only called Ann to their house to clean up, bring chopped wood in, or wash dishes. Ann's mom was livid.

Ann's mom said, "Since you are looking for a maid and not a granddaughter, Ann won't be back."

Ann remembered her mother screaming, "Call some of your other grandchildren that live up North because you're done treating Ann like a slave."

She looked at Ann and said, "Let's go."

Ann never saw or heard from them again.

When her father died, Ann went to Carowinds, and when his mother died, she went to Six Flags. Ann never developed a real relationship with him or his family. They were simply neighbors three doors down around the corner from her. She spoke just like she did with all the other neighbors in passing. They never accepted Ann, so she wasn't going to stop her plans to attend her grandmother's or father's funeral. They'd been dead to her well before the funerals ever got scheduled. She doesn't remember when his father died. Ann's dad gave her fifteen dollars in the fifteen years of her life. She didn't feel as though she had a relationship with any of them. They were just connected by blood.

***

"Geesh. The storm is back," I thought.

I'm glad I don't live in a flood zone because, with all this rain, my house and I would probably already float away.

I heard the voice of the Lord say, "Focus!"

"Yes, Lord," I replied.

Ann's emotions were becoming overwhelming to the point I could no longer tell the difference between her thoughts and my own. It seemed as though I was experiencing these emotions as Ann.

"Please, God. This is affecting me," I said. "I can barely type because of how Ann feels. Her pain, anger, and sorrow have become mine. Please, God, I beg of you to let this cup pass from me. I feel like Jesus praying in the Garden of Gethsemane."

I hear "write." I take a deep breath and begin to type.

***

In another memory, Ann appears to be approximately six years old. Ann's mom pulled into her grandmother's yard to pick her up for a doctor's appointment. Her mom went into the house to get her grandmother. While inside, she asked her brother, "Can you watch Ann until we come back?"

He replied, "Yes."

No sooner than they pulled out of the yard, he immediately put Ann down for a nap. Ann's eyes welled up as I watched what happened next. Her uncle went and got into bed with her. He took her panties off and began to rub around her private area with his hand. He then took his penis and began rubbing up and down Ann's private area without penetrating.

Ann laughed and said, "That tickles."

After about two hours, he heard her mother pull back in the yard and whispered, "Don't tell anyone this is a game that only you and I will play."

He put her panties back on and reminded her of their secret, explaining no one would understand. He went into the bathroom while she walked to get in the car.

Ann skips ahead approximately nine years to a memory where she is now about fifteen years old. She and some of her family members are sitting outside on the porch at her aunt and uncle's house. She was playing but was close enough to hear her mom and a couple of other family members talking about a cousin who was being molested by her father. It made her so uncomfortable. They went into detail about what was supposed to have happened. That night, she began to have what seemed like dreams of something similar happening to her. She thought it was just a terrible nightmare that she just kept having because she was afraid it would happen to her. Finally, the dreams started coming as she lay wide awake. She realized they were not dreams but memories. Ann went to her mother and told her that it had happened and by whom. She looked at Ann, never saying a word, and changed the subject. It was never spoken of again.

***

With tears running down my face, I watched as this little girl cried. I decided to try to see who she was. The closer I got to her, the more I could feel her hurt and the suffering she faced. This time, I was determined to see who she was. I wanted to help her if I could. As I walked around her, I realized the little girl was me. I was just as vulnerable and insecure now as she was then. We are the same. God commissioned me to tell my own story through the innocent eyes of Ann. God used the little girl in me to unlock the beginning of our journey to Him. I am Robin Annette Wages, and this is my story.

I suffered many traumas in my life; however, Ann was the first victim—the beginning of my downward spiral that led to my messed-up life today. She was the most vulnerable because she was a child and couldn't comprehend why these terrible things happened. She pushed her feelings deep down inside of her and forgot about them.

However, as an adult, I grew tired and wanted a better life, but I simply didn't know how to accomplish it. Therefore, God sent me back through Ann to reveal the things I had long forgotten. I believe that I was so busy trying to survive during that time that I never stopped to look at the specifics. Life can become a blur when living in survival mode, but the more I wrote, the more I remembered. That's why the images weren't always clear, and I could only see from behind or behind her eyes. I believe my desire to help her was driven by my unconscious connection to her and her life. Trauma is hard for any adult, but through the eyes of a child, it can be completely devastating.

As I look back, I disassociated myself from my pain. It was the only way I could survive constant trauma. My desire was to help Ann, but when I found out that it was me, I felt helpless and vulnerable, just as Ann did all those years ago. Something in me was unlocked, and for the first time, I cried, mourning for the little girl in me. As a little girl, what happened to me was not my fault; however, the trauma of it devastated me. I didn't know that what I went through was trauma. In fact, it looked normal, based on what I was used to seeing and hearing. However, the traumas I went through as a child was the foundation that led to an out-of-control downward spiral that was quickly becoming my life. I now had to deal with issues I had buried long ago. So, God used through the eyes of a child to reveal my truth.

This chapter is simply about acknowledging your trauma. The pain was so great that I buried it deep within me. Through this chapter, God reminded me of things that I had long forgotten. This process could look different based on the person and or their situation. However, God remains the same. If He starts you down the path, He will never leave you. For me, the process of becoming free took almost twenty years. God had me to process every trauma as I typed. There were weeks, months, and even years that I was unable to move on.

I need you to understand my process was the most painful, messy thing I ever went through because I had to put my needs before the needs of the people who hurt me or even how people felt about what I was going through or even doing. So, I ask you today, are you ready to acknowledge your trauma, which is the first step in getting free of the bondage that has held you and your life hostage?

CHAPTER TWO

The 2nd Hour: Who Am I?

I cannot say that my next few years were any easier as a teenager. I thank God that every day wasn't bad, but there were enough of them. I knew what was happening but did not understand why it was happening. It seemed life had chosen me to punish, and I was confused and angry about it. I didn't have what I needed to figure things out. I constantly stayed in trouble because I was considered mean. People say I have always been that way. My earliest memory of being mean was the day my mother gave my easy bake oven to a cousin. I was between the ages of 8 and 10. I was so mad I pushed her down, and a nail went through her foot. I didn't care and didn't bother to check on her. I simply picked up my easy bake oven and went home. I thought my mom was going to kill me. After I got my behind cut, she made me take it right back. I think that mentality followed me through life. Now, don't get me wrong, I didn't bother anyone, but it wasn't good for you to bother me, either. I didn't mince words and would fight at the drop of a dime. You see, I grew up a Tom Boy. As a teenager, I remember playing basketball so aggressively until I hit my wrist against the pole and had a big knot. It was black and blue. I also remember playing tackle football with my cousins and getting hit so hard that they knocked the wind out of me. The buttons even came loose on my shirt, so my cousin gave me his shirt to put on to finish the game. Finally, while playing "Evil Knievel," my cousin and I set up a ramp, and I got up to a good speed, jumping and then spinning the bike in a semi-circle while leaning it over. I literally pulled all the skin off my hip. I will never forget that day my mom made a bath for me with alcohol. When I got in that tub, I yelled and tried to jump out, but she held me down. I also remember running down a dirt road with no shoes on.

There were three girls and about twelve boys in my neighborhood. We stayed out from sunup to sundown. No one thought about sex or anything of that nature. This was during the time that if you did something wrong around the corner up the street, by the time you got home, your mother was calling for you to get your butt cut, or at least that's what I heard. I tried my best to stay out of sight and off everyone's mind; that way, I didn't have to be around the drama or be reminded of what happened. I hung out all day and half the night until it was time to eat, take a bath, and go to bed. Finally, life was good, if only for a while.

I was now 15 years old, 5'3 and 129 lbs. The ponytails were gone, and I had shoulder-length hair. My body had developed, and I had the attention of the boys. This was a big change because before, I was everyone's sister. Now I was fine as they used to say, Hmm... I may have changed physically, but trust me, my mom wasn't playing those types of games. She made it clear a long time ago: no sex, no drinking, no smoking, and don't go to jail. The tone in her voice let me know she was not playing, and I was not going to try her.

This was also a time when we went to church a lot. I was beginning to experience adolescence and all the problems that come along with it. Peer pressure was tough. You see, all my friends were partying and having sex, or at least that's what they said. As for me, I was scared to death of my mother. I did not have a mother that played those types of games. She worked hard to take care of me and my sister, so pregnancy or any kind of trouble was out of the question. However, I was searching for something I would never find in human flesh, but believe me, I eventually found the courage to try.

There was never a Sunday that we did not go to church. Truthfully, I loved going to church because I loved the singing. OMG, I could stay at the church revival or usher board anniversaries all day long. At my childhood church, when revivals came, people loaded their cars with all types of food. Each person would park, open their trunks, and serve the food between the morning service and the revival starts. We went from one trunk to the next. Everybody shared. Once the eating was over, we all went back to the church and enjoyed Jesus. At times, there were 20-plus choirs in attendance. No one was getting up to leave early. No one was looking at their watch. All you could see was hands clapping, feet patting, and people rocking and singing. That was on Sunday. The problem was what I heard on Sunday and what I saw Monday through Saturday were two completely different things. I didn't know how to take the words out of the Bible and apply them to my life. I wanted to know the God that I heard people singing about. I heard stories out of the Bible, but how do I make those stories work in real life to build my faith? I honestly could not remember anyone who read the Bible and did what it said. If the older people couldn't do it, how in the world could I? I guess this is where I started making bad decisions and not understanding and recognizing my purpose or worth in life. I could feel deep within me that something was missing, but I honestly had no clue what it was. A pattern started to emerge, and I felt hopeless about getting past what I was feeling without an intervention from God or at least who I thought He was. The truth is, my body had grown; I had gotten older in age but not in my thinking. It was time for me to grow up.

***

The days of my youth spilled over into adolescent life. God made an appearance that day while I was sitting on my mother's couch, but I had not heard from Him since, or at least that's what I thought. Once I saw how the world worked, I just didn't have the strength to buck against it. I guess I accepted it as normal and tried to go with it. I learned to endure silently. There was only one option in my family, and that was to be strong and suck it up. However, deep within, I felt like I was dying. I learned never to talk about anything that brought shame and embarrassment to the family, even if that thing was detrimental to me. I did everything I could not to think about what happened. Every time thoughts and feelings would emerge, I blamed myself, and I rehearsed how I could and should have protected myself. It was too much. As I look back, God was literally beginning to peel back the layers of my life, but I had no clue of all I had to go through in order to see that God was my solution. I wanted to know about the God I heard about on Sundays. He was loving and kind, and He also took care of His people. He constantly delivered them even when they got themselves into a mess. It was a love I wanted to experience. However, I had no example, so I had to figure it out on my own.

I started a journey that would take me a lifetime to comprehend, embrace, and return. His love was different from what I was used to. It was strange to me, and I wasn't sure if I could be good enough for Him to love me. Trust me, I had plenty of reasons to be disqualified from Him loving me. I was broken and damaged by people who said they loved me. I heard about the love of God but didn't see it in any of His people.

I remember that day well; my grandmother passed away, and we were preparing for the funeral. I remember being at the church and people crying and throwing up. I was so confused. This was a woman that I was not going to miss. She treated me so badly, and I knew I was not the only one. However, they were heartbroken by her death. All I could honestly remember thinking was, "Ding dong. The witch is dead."

We were fierce as a family during these times. We had our nice clothes on, hair fried, died, and laid to the side. Can you say casket sharp? We put our differences aside and paid our respects. However, once the service was over, we went back to doing what we did so well, raising hell.

I remember one day, my aunt Rudy and one of my cousins (Patty) got into a physical fight over who knows what. Surprisingly, everyone was standing around watching. I remember running over to break them up, but I remember thinking of how it all felt so wrong and that we had sunken to a new low. This had become the norm for our family, and deep within, it scared me because I was raised to respect my elders. How could they be fighting? This disturbed me greatly. I do believe that I was very naïve when it came to life. I think I wanted to believe that people were good. Remember when I talked about how I felt like I was different? Deep down in me, I did not want to believe that people were mean and hateful as I had seen growing up. How I felt was not based on experience but simply a gut feeling. I guess I had to learn the hard way, which started me on this crazy path that became my life.

***

I do not remember his name now, but this was my first introduction to sex in a relationship. It was three months before I graduated high school. This would have been around March of 1987, and I was still a virgin and had never been kissed. I was considered a late bloomer because my friends had been actively sexual for years, or at least that is what they said. I finally decided I was ready and had my eyes set on this guy I had been liking for quite a while. He really seemed to like me as well, right up until I did the do, and he was gone. Let's just say we graduated, and I moved on to the next. I didn't realize it at the time, but a pattern was forming. For every season that changed, it began with a new guy. This was the beginning of a new kind of self-inflicted downward spiral.

Don't get me wrong, I wasn't jumping from man to man having sex. I would be in a relationship for about six months before even considering it. The funny part is they would wait and then leave. I was learning a lesson about men but was too blind to see or acknowledge the games that were being played.

Then I met this nice guy named Daniel. After graduation, I started working in a gas station that was close to his neighborhood. We talked when he would come in, eventually exchanging numbers, and we began to call each other and hang out. He was truly a dream come true. He was 6 ft tall, light-skinned, thin with short black wavy hair. He had a great personality. He also worked hard. Daniel was a man. I'm talking about a real man, not a boy pretending to be a man. I really don't think I ever saw him down. He was always smiling and full of life. He moved as if everything he said or did had a purpose, even being with me. Daniel wasn't like the other guys I knew. Looking back, I really could have spent the rest of my life with this man. My experience with men was very limited at this point, and I was too young to settle down, and he understood that. He said and did all the right things, but I was simply too young.

Daniel treated me like there was no one else in the world besides me. My friends used to tell me horror stories about their relationships, but for me, life was starting to look pretty good. God finally had sent me something special. I literally had no complaints. Trust me, after this last guy, Daniel was a breath of fresh air. We did everything together, it seemed. He understood that I was young, but he still treated me in a special way.

Now, Daniel was about seven years older than me. That would make me about 17 and him 24. He dressed nice and smelled so good. I was in heaven! Daniel also worked full-time for a construction company. This man worked like he wanted to be something, and because I still lived at home, he would call my mom and ask if it was okay for him to take me out. She always said yes. I guess she trusted him.

I remember one day, he needed me to pick up the payroll for his crew because he was working out of town. When I got there, he put me and my girlfriend up in a hotel. He stayed with me, and my girlfriend stayed with his friend whom she liked. The truth is we seldom slept together, but that night was different, and our relationship went to another level. I believe he learned that though I was young, he could depend on and trust me if the need arose.

Daniel exposed me to things I had never done before, such as driving his truck, which was a straight shift, and riding a motorcycle. I remember him even showing me how to read plans on how to build buildings. He wanted me to think about what I eventually wanted to do in life. He really cared about me because, honestly, he could have had me any time he wanted, but he was more interested in my mind and my dreams. I know it sounds corny, but it's true. As I said, he was older, and he was different.

As I think about him now, Daniel really showed me how a man was supposed to treat a woman. There were times I would be hanging with friends, and he would stop by and pick me and all my friends up and take us out to nice restaurants. Not McDonald's or Burger King, but places like Applebee's. I think we went to California Dreaming once. To me, it was something I could never afford on my own at this stage in my life. Daniel footed the bill for all of us, never complaining or demanding anything in return. I remember one day, I needed money to pay a bill, and he signed a blank check and said to fill in the amount for whatever I needed. That's the type of man he was.

I guess you're wondering what happened to Daniel. He had a crazy ex-girlfriend that would not leave him alone. Remember I told you I was fine, but the mindset wasn't right. I thought I was fine enough to pull another one just like him. Yep, I walked away.

Looking back, Daniel was everything I needed physically but nothing I needed spiritually. We went everywhere together except church. He could give me everything I wanted and nothing I needed. You see, Daniel was my second attempt at finding love. He was a perfect distraction for a 17-year-old girl who was naïve and fresh out of school, stepping into a world she knew nothing about.

I honestly would not encourage this type of relationship looking back because I spent the rest of my life looking for someone who would treat me the way Daniel did. I was very impressionable and incapable of processing what I had or how it would affect my life in the days to come. I was happy but still on my way to hell. The devil doesn't always show up in red with a tail, horns, and a cape. He can also come tall, nice, and sweet, smelling good with the best intentions.

***

I started working full-time right after getting out of school. I wanted to try and get my own place, not to mention Aunt Rudy said that she would get me a car, but I would need to make the payments and maintain it. I started working at McDonald's but just wasn't making enough money to do all I needed it to. I spoke with my mom, who in turn talked to Aunt Rudy, who was the supervisor over the mess hall on Fort Jackson. It was agreed that I would go and work there full time and continue McDonalds part-time. My schedule was crazy.

Sunday was all-day church. I sang in the choir and served on the usher board. Monday-Friday—Mess Hall 5 am - 1 pm and McDonald's—5 pm -10 pm. I worked every other Saturday from 5 pm - 10 pm. I must admit, the days were long, but it kept me busy. Daniel quickly faded to the back of my mind, and the desire to party set in.

My friends and I decided that we wanted to try out the clubs on base. Shelby and I would get dressed and head out the door to be met by her sister Wendy, saying I'm going with you. Shelby and I would look at each other and bust out laughing. She would look so sad we would say come on.

Once on base, we would have to stand in line until an officer would sign us in. It wouldn't take long before someone we would know would come by, and before you know it, we were in. We would party from 10 pm - 3 am, Fridays and Saturdays. We would go so much until they knew us and would just sign us in until the day I got busted. You see, I worked on the same army base I partied on, so the soldiers kind of knew me. One day, while working the line and serving food, an officer came through and asked, "Don't I know you?"

I looked and said, "No, I don't think so."

He said, "I know, I know you. I just don't know where from."

I didn't look up and continued to serve the other soldiers.

He scratched his head but walked away to sit down and eat. I didn't know this man outside of the mess hall.

Then, one day, officer Tattletale came in while I was setting up the food line, walked over to my mom, and asked, "Who is that?"

My mom said, "Oh, that's my daughter."

He said, "Are you serious? I know her."

She said, "No, you can't know her. How would you have met her?"

He said, "She comes in on Saturday to the Officers club, and we sign her in. She is wild."

I could have fallen through the floor.

My mom yelled, "What!"

I looked back at Officer Tattletale and rolled my eyes.

When I got in the kitchen, my mom soon followed and said, "Oh, so you're partying on base? That's over!"

I said, "Yes, ma'am." Then, I went back to work.

***

I still continued to work hard but had to find another place to party because of Officer Tattletale. Boy, he messed up a good thing. However, I had no regrets because we met some really cool people who became friends. All the partying took my mind off relationships, or should I say the lack of being in one.

One day, while hanging out with friends at my part-time job (McDonald's), I noticed a man about 5'6, slim, red, and very smooth in his conversation who was with some of his friends. I noticed that he kept watching me, so I smiled. He got up and came over to introduce himself as Jeff. After talking for a few minutes, he asked for my number, and the rest is history. I mean, I worked so much; what would be the chance of something coming out of this? He would be good as a homeboy. However, it didn't work out that way. He became very persistent, and we ended up dating. Jeff didn't meet Daniels's standard, but hey, maybe I can change him, I thought. The problem was I really didn't know who this man was. There is a movie called "Sleeping with the Enemy," and well, I was. I just didn't know it. We dated long enough for us to become engaged. I guess once that happened, the real him came out. Jeff was on drugs bad. I don't know how I didn't know. However, now that I think about it, I don't remember him ever going to work or taking me anywhere to do anything. I, on the other hand, was working a full-time and part-time job and singing on the usher board every Sunday. I knew what I was doing was wrong, but it was what everyone was doing. Besides, he said he loved me; in fact, he loved me enough to give me a ring and ask me to be his wife.

I began to see many inconsistencies with Jeff and, therefore, never set a date. I had already started having second thoughts when it happened. Jeff asked if he could borrow my car to handle some business while I was at work. Long story short, he got arrested, and my car was impounded. I contacted the jail to see what I needed to do to get my car released. Jeff said that he would not release my keys out of his property without me getting him out. I sucked it up and went to my dear sweet grandmother for the money. She gave me a lecture but lent me the money. I went and paid the bond, and he released my keys. This was it for me; my mind was made up, and I was returning his ring. The next day, I went by his apartment while my girlfriend waited in the car. I explained why the engagement was over and that I was done seeing him.

Jeff grabbed me and said, "I'm not letting you go."

We struggled, and I fell. Jeff began to drag me up the steps to his bedroom. I continued to fight until he stopped dragging and decided to make his point right there on the steps.

As he penetrated me, he whispered in my ear, "If I can't have you, no one will because I'm going to fill you up with babies."

I whispered back to him with tears running down my face, "You may enjoy putting it there, but I will enjoy killing it!"

Jeff rolled off me, looking strange, as if I had said something crazy. He went upstairs, and I pulled my panties and pants up, placed the ring on his mantle, and left. When I returned to the car, tears were running down my face. I told my girlfriend he raped me. She wanted to call the police.

"Please don't," I begged. "I placed myself in that situation, and I deserved what happened."

Jeff did not leave me with a baby. Instead, he left me with three sexually transmitted diseases that I wouldn't find out about for years. Years later, I saw an article in the paper about Jeff. He had a lot of kids sitting on the bench beside a young lady trying to get public assistance at the local Department of Social Services. I thought about how my life would have turned out if I didn't get out. However, truthfully, I was mad as hell for what he did to me all those years ago. I had already come from a crazy family, been molested, and now add a rape, not to mention three sexually transmitted diseases. I was losing it. I remember seeing Jeff several years after I got married. At this point in my life, I was truly trying to develop a relationship with God. I was a born-again believer, and I guess it was time for my faith to be tested. I will never forget the day Jeff walked into the jail where I worked. I had put on weight, so he didn't know who I was; however, I recognized him immediately. He kept looking at me, saying he knew me, and I would say, "No, you don't." I escorted him to his unit and forgot about it. For approximately two months straight, I believe I worked his dorm on my regular scheduled days and overtime.

Finally, I prayed and asked God, "Why?"

God said, "It's time you released it!"

I begged and pleaded with God to no avail.

I said, "God, if it's your will, then give me the opportunity."

The next day, he was in the dorm by himself, asleep. He got up to see what officer was working the dorm. It was the trustee dorm, so inmates were always coming and going to work.

Once again, he said, "I know I know you."

I took a deep breath and said, "Yes, you do, or at least you did."

I went on to tell him what he had done to me and how it affected my life. When I looked up, tears were rolling down his face, and he began to apologize.

He said, "I am so sorry, and I promise I will never hurt another woman the way I hurt you."

I replied, "I was humiliated to contract three sexually transmitted diseases from a man I was engaged to be married to."

I went on to explain how it also affected my daughter. He wanted to know how it affected her.

I said, "Cara's lungs weren't completely developed, so the doctors had to give her steroids, and she developed slower than other kids, which caused her to struggle in school. Every time I look at her, I am reminded of the decision I made to be with you. It is all my fault that she struggles, all because I trusted you. I wasn't your girlfriend or side chick; I was engaged to be your wife!"

Jeff said, "I'm sorry, but can we start over."

I said, "No way. Now return to your bunk."

Jeff walked out of the office, and we never spoke again. When I returned to work, he had been released, and I never saw or heard from him again. I'm exhausted, so I think I will just go to sleep and start fresh in the morning. Maybe the sun will come out tomorrow, and I can walk in the bright sunshine. I'm tired of this rain. A sunny day, from my mouth to God's ears. I turned the lights out, curled up in the bed, closed my eyes, whispered, "Thank you, Jesus," and fell asleep.

***

Morning came quickly. I got up, whispered a short prayer, and made a cup of coffee. Lord knows I need it. However, overall, I felt refreshed as I thought I would. As I sat looking out the window, I saw that the storm had passed, at least for now. I went outside to see what damage had been done, and to my amazement, everything was still intact. I said a little prayer of gratitude and began to plan out my day. There were some things I needed to take care of today. However, God's will come first. My assignment was to write. As I thought about this last season of this chapter, I prayed that my message was clear. I was looking for me.

I tried to be many things to many people. My heart was in it for the right reasons, but I still came out with the same result. Through this journey, I see the pitfalls the enemy placed in my life and how I walked into them. I was looking for love and acceptance in all the wrong places. Now I'm sure that I cannot be the only person to do this. The truth is, I looked for it in men, whereas others may use drugs or alcohol. We all have a vice in some way, shape, or form. However, for me, I decided that if I were going to get screwed, it would be on my own terms. I became this heartless, bitter person. Somewhere along the road, I lost my smile. I was tired. By this time, I was contemplating suicide because no matter how hard I tried, I couldn't break the cycle. No, I hadn't tried anything, but it was a continuous thought. To be honest, I was disgusted with living but was more afraid to die. I remembered sitting on the side of the bed, begging God to take my life. I wanted to go home with Him where I knew it had to be better than where I was. This last relationship felt so real but was wrong. I wish I could say this was the last time this type of thing happened to me, but it wasn't.

***

One day, while working at Burger King, my manager's friend came through the door. This man was fine. He was slightly taller than me, light-skinned, and well-groomed. Lord, this man smelled good and looked good. Now, this time, I wasn't interested in a relationship. I just wanted a "cut buddy" no-strings-attached kind of deal. It wasn't long before we were in the sheets. Philip and I hooked up maybe three times, and he disappeared. He had finished school and went back to his hometown. I ended up with a terrible discharge some months later and had to go to the emergency room. My cousin decided to go with me to see what was up. The doctors ran a series of tests. Well, turns out that I was pregnant. I asked the doctor to run the test three times. Each time, the results were the same "positive." Though I was a young adult, I was still in my mother's house, and she was going to kill me. I didn't go home; I went to my aunt's house to drop my cousin off.

As soon as I walked through the door, my aunt asked, "What did they say?"

I replied, "I'm pregnant."

"Are you going to tell the father?" My aunt asked.

I said, "No, because we weren't in a relationship."

She replied, "At least give him a chance to do the right thing."

I prayed that she wouldn't tell my mom. I needed time to break it to her. After a few weeks, I finally told her, and she said she wasn't doing anything for me or my child. The tears rolled down my face because she was so cruel and mean to me. I could tell in her voice she meant every word. The next seven months were hell in that house. So, I worked all the time to build my bank to get my own place. If I was home, I was sleeping or getting ready to go to work. I was 19 years old and pregnant; what in the world was I going to do? I decided to take my aunt up on her advice.

I called Phillip and told him I needed to talk to him. We decided to meet at my job. I explained that I was pregnant.

He said, "Who is the daddy?"

I looked at him and said, "You."

He stared as though I could be lying. So, I said, "I guess it's me." I turned and walked away, not saying a word.

I immediately began to prepare to make a life for myself and my baby. The pregnancy was hard. I started having cramps that indicated I was trying to miscarry. I ended up going to the emergency room, where they told me I needed to slow down working and turn on my left side when the pain started. I had a lot to accomplish, so I continued to work, took breaks as needed, and tried to eat healthily for the sake of my baby.

Now, if you can remember, Phillip and I were not in a serious relationship but what people called cut buddies. Meaning we hooked up whenever the need arose. Therefore, when I told him I was pregnant, he didn't believe me. We ended up parting ways until he showed up after I turned 4 months pregnant.

He rubbed my stomach and said, "Wow, you are really pregnant?"

"Yes," I said.

Even though we were cut buddies, I would never sleep with more than one man at a time for that very reason.

He said, "Okay, I will be back before the baby is born."

When I turned 7 months pregnant, I went to my doctor for a checkup. My baby had been measuring small, but today, something was wrong. I had been having really bad headaches and gained one hundred pounds in 7 months. I assumed it was me working so much mixed with the pregnancy. My doctor entered the room and quickly exited.

When my doctor returned, he said, "You're being admitted."

I said, "No, wait. I have something to do. Can I leave and come back?"

He replied, "No, this is life or death. What is the phone number of your next of kin?"

I gave him my mother and sister's number, and then I was taken upstairs to labor and delivery.

My sister was the first to show up because my mom couldn't be reached. They told her that I had Preeclampsia and that both our lives were in jeopardy. My sister immediately contacted my mom's head office, who tracked her down and told her she needed to get to the hospital immediately. Once there, I overheard the doctor tell my mom that she needed to choose because there was a high probability that only one of us would make it. I was scared because I didn't know who she would choose. We weren't on the best of terms.

I was prepped and given a labor inducer early in the morning on July 11, around 8 am. I still hadn't gone into labor by 5 pm that day. My mom came in and spoke with the doctor. The decision was made for me to have a Cesarean. Approximately 20 minutes after the surgery started, Cara was born at 3lbs 6oz. She was described by my mom as looking like a necktie (long and skinny). I was now out of jeopardy, but Cara had a way to go because her lungs weren't fully developed. Her first feedings were from an eye dropper. The milk was dropped on her tongue because her jaw wasn't strong enough to suck milk out of a bottle. She remained in the hospital for about a month because of her weight and inability to eat. After I was released, I went back and forth to the hospital to feed her. My mom finally got tired and started going to the hospital to get Cara to suck milk from a bottle. Every time we would go, she would gain a pound, and the next day, she would lose the pound. My mom contacted the doctor and told them that Cara was being discharged that day. Although the doctor didn't think it was a good idea, the doctor agreed because of my mom's persistence. My mom sent me to sign the papers while she dressed Cara. Within an hour, Cara was headed home. My mom set the rules for me and everyone that visited.

She then said, "Use a pillow to hold her because Cara is so small; the pillow would ensure no one drops her."

My mom took responsibility for everything concerning Cara. She slept with her, fed her, dressed her, and took her to the doctor. Whatever Cara needed, my mom did it. I had to ask permission to take my baby anywhere or to do anything with her.

She would bring Cara to me in the mornings when she was on her way to work.

Her word to me was, "Do not roll over her. If you do, you better be out of the state of South Carolina before I get home."

My mom started Cara on milk for the first week and introduced cereal one week later. Before I knew it, Cara was up to 5lbs and thriving within a month.

Cara was 3 months old when I saw Phillip again, then again at 6 months, and finally at 18 years, when they continued their own relationship. To his defense, I found out after Cara was grown that he and his family came down several times to see her, but my mother threatened to shoot them if they ever returned.

He said, "I did the best I could with child support, having other children, eight more to be exact."

I said, "I never received child support."

He replied, "They went to your mom's house."

I thought the story was farfetched, but my mother confirmed and said, "Cara didn't need them; she had us." But my mom cashed every check, never even telling me they were coming. This caused all kinds of problems between Cara and me and between Cara and her dad.

Phillip was just another attempt to gain control over a life that was slowly spinning out of control. Every round may go higher and higher, but with every relationship, I sunk lower and lower.

I'm sure by now you can see that a pattern was well underway. However, I need and want you to see what the devil was doing to me beneath the surface. He had started stacking the deck against me. From the time of my youth up until this point, I had sunken into a deep hole that I wasn't sure I would get out of. Every encounter left something behind. The men were gone, but the spirits weren't. I want to keep this part as simple as I can because someone reading may not understand. Every time you have sex with someone, an exchange takes place—they deposit something into you. I need you to understand that all I saw and experienced in my family left me starving for affection and a sense of wanting to fit in. These relationships opened me up to the devil! Yes, you heard me, the devil! So, I began to struggle more than I ever thought I would.

I was in trouble, and this time, I knew only God could get me out. Unfortunately, I confused God with church folks. Big mistake. It was time for me to find out who

God truly was. I had a lot to learn, and Lord knows I wasn't prepared for any of it.

***

I saw Daniel some years later.

He asked, "Can I stop by?"

I told him, "Yes, it would be nice to catch up."

Daniel was now the owner of two construction companies and eight apartment buildings.

He said, "God has truly blessed me." He went on to say he married his crazy ex because she wasn't going to allow him to be with anyone else, and they had two children together. Unfortunately, his wife died, and there was now another young lady helping him and the children get through their loss. He was so confused.

I told him, "Take some time. Just because the funeral is over doesn't mean you've finished grieving." I went on to say, "It sounds as though this other young lady is in love with you. You need to take it slow and decide how you feel about her."

He paused for a moment, then said, "Will you have my daughter? You won't ever want for anything again. I don't ever want to get married again because I never want to experience that kind of hurt again."

I nodded and asked, "The hurt you experienced losing your wife?"

He added, "Yes, you would have everything except the paper."

I took a deep breath and said, "No. I'm sorry but I'm not having any more children."

Daniel walked over, hugged me, and walked out the door, walking out of my life forever!

Reflections

Looking back, I see that God was showing me the areas where I needed help. You see, it's not enough to know that you have an issue; you must identify what the issues are in order to correct the behavior. This was the beginning of a long list of things that I needed to be delivered from. However, this chapter deals with looking for love in the faces of men. I know now that the love I was looking for would never be found in a man or even a woman. I needed the love of God, but at this point, I was clueless and continued on my destructive path. So, my question to you today is, what are you looking for in man (people) that only God can give you?

CHAPTER THREE

The 3rd Hour: God Who are You?

I was now a 20-year-old with an infant. I needed a job that paid a little more, so I started working at Burger King and continued working at Fort Jackson Meps. My mom decided she would keep Cara while I worked because she was born premature. My goals were set, and I was working toward getting my own place, which would provide stability for Cara.

Adrian and I started working the same shift and realized we went to the same school, but he was a year behind me. He was that guy friend that every girl dreamed of. You know that friend that you could depend on, and you never had to worry about whether you liked each other in that way. We were buddies, just hanging out and trying to deal with the crazy stuff going on in our lives.

One day, after my daughter's father was long gone, I noticed that things had somehow changed between us. I think that we had spent so much time together until feelings crept in, to both of our surprise. Adrian knew everything about me because, in the beginning, we were the best of friends, so there was no reason to hold back or even lie because our relationship wasn't based on love or any kind of affection. He was my homeboy. In the days following, we noticed awkward moments that had never happened before. Finally, we talked about it and wanted to see where it would lead.

The truth is nothing changed for quite a while until the day he and I decided to take the relationship to the next level—we decided to move in together. However, the place we were looking at was a little more than we could afford, so I asked a mutual friend if she wanted to move with us. She agreed, and we moved into this beautiful three-bedroom mobile home. There was only one problem, that place was roach-infested. I don't know why we didn't see them when we looked at the place, but the day we got the key, they were in full effect. I knew we couldn't move our stuff in before bombing the place. We bought about thirty roach bombs and set them off all over the house. When we came back the next day, we honestly couldn't see the floor because of the dead roaches. They were in the cabinets, on the countertops, and in the tubs. All I could do was gag as we started to clean them up. After all three of us got to do some substantial cleaning, we were ready to move in. Life was good. Adrian felt more relaxed in the days to come. His mom decided she wanted to get him a car so that he could get back and forth to work and so that he would be able to come see her. You see, all of us were sharing my car when we moved together. Our schedules were starting to get a little hectic, so another car was a plus. However, it caused more problems between Adrian and his stepfather. I'm not sure as to what happened, but the car was on the verge of being repossessed. Adrian was so stressed when he talked to me about it that I said I would help him. We pooled our money together and saved the car. I believe that this was when Adrian first realized that I was in for the long run. It really drew us closer together than we had ever imagined.

Now, I haven't said anything about sex because I honestly don't remember anything about it. I'm not saying it was bad or good; it's just at this point in my life, I was learning what it was to be in a real relationship. To truly depend on another person and have them depend on you. We were making it work.

Now, at this time, my daughter was living with my mother. She wanted her to stay in a stable environment until Adrian and I could figure out what we were doing. Truth is, I was working so much until it was just easier for her to be with my mom. I made sure she had everything she needed, but deep within me, I wasn't happy with the way things were. I didn't feel right having my mom take care of my daughter. She was mine, and I wanted her with me. I saw Cara every day, and she stayed with me every weekend, but it simply was just not enough. So, I started dropping hints to Adrian that I wanted my daughter at the house with us. I don't think he understood what I meant. He said he understood, but no sooner than I brought her to live with us did our problems start. I quickly realized that he wasn't interested in being a dad to Cara, so we all moved back in with our parents, and I applied for housing and food stamps.

We continued to see each other when we could, but my primary focus was to get everything ready so that when housing called, I would be ready. I needed furniture, linen, dishes, washcloths, towels, etc. If you could name it, I needed it. We divided everything from the mobile home; therefore, I had to ensure I had everything I would need to take care of my daughter. I stayed in the club on Friday and Saturday nights. I would wait until Cara went to sleep, which was generally around 10 pm. After that, it was party over here and party over there.

Adrian called and said he needed to talk to me. Things at his house were getting worse, and he didn't know what to do. He and his stepfather were arguing daily, and his mother was in the middle of it all. He showed up later that night after he got off work, and we talked for hours. It seemed his stepfather wanted him out of the house, but he had no place to go. I guess we both got caught up in the moment and started to have sex right there in my mom's house. We were so involved until my mom walked in on us.

My mom said, “It's time that you move.”

I agreed.

Adrian asked my mom, "If we got married, could I move in with you guys until we find something else?"

"Yes," my mother replied.

We went down and got married within the next two days. I wasn't happy about moving with my mom, not even as a newlywed. However, we paid rent of $500 a month and bought our own groceries to help her out. It was also good because Adrian handled cutting the grass and minor repairs that needed to be done.

Within six months, housing called, and we had our own 3-bedroom apartment. The problem was that Adrian, now my husband, and mother had no idea I was taking my baby with me. As I began to pack to get ready for the move, they realized that I wasn't just packing our stuff but Cara's stuff as well. Both began to question me about why I was moving her when she had been in that house for so long.

I simply said, "Because I am her mother, and she needs to be with me."

It did not go over well with either of them. My mom was furious with me, but Adrian tried to understand and make it work. Things went fine for a while, but you could feel the tension building. Adrian didn't want the responsibility of taking care of a child, especially when there was a responsible adult who was ready and willing to take on the responsibility. However, I knew that she was my responsibility and refused to budge. We went on day after day, growing more and more apart. The conversation or, should I say, arguments became so intense until we became two people living in a house, sharing the financial responsibility. I became desperate because, in all honesty, I loved him but saw where we were headed. How could he expect me to walk away from my child for him? I had spent the first nine years of her life away, visiting in between jobs. I needed to be a part of her life, and she needed me just as much. What am I going to do? Why should I have to choose between the man I love and my own daughter? I couldn't come to terms with the fact that this was the way it was going to be. How could God allow such a thing to happen? The problem grew beyond my ability to handle it. This was my second real thought of suicide. I remember sitting on the side of the bed, begging God to take my life. I reasoned that maybe Cara would be better off with my mom, and Adrian could finally move on and be with someone who doesn't have a child. Everyone would win.

As I thought about it, I heard a voice within myself say, "Girl, you are saved! Suicide is not an option!"

Besides, black people don't kill themselves, at least not intentionally. We may work ourselves to death but not intentionally take our own life. I smiled and got ready for work. I knew that suicide wasn't an option, but I still needed to find a solution. I realized that every Sunday, we sat at home watching one game or another. I decided to get back into church. I would get Cara and me ready and head to church, praying that this would eventually help me with my marriage. I really tried not to get into any arguments because I wanted God to move on my behalf. I also stopped going to the club and tried to focus on making my marriage work. I really wanted us to become a real family. In my mind, if it didn't work, it wouldn't be because I didn't try everything.

After attending church for about three months, I got up enough nerve to talk to my pastor about what was going on. I told him that if something did not change soon, I just didn't believe our marriage would recover.

Pastor responded, "Invite him to church. Maybe if he felt a part of something, he would understand why family is so important."

Adrian came, and we started going to the marriage ministry. Things seemed to be getting better right up until the time the pastor attacked him concerning what I told him. He never went to another service with me. In fact, I never remember him going back to a church service with me other than a funeral.

Cara was close to two of her cousins, and they used to spend the night quite often. I guess because they were so close in age, they wanted to be together all the time. I would let Cara go with them sometimes, but mostly, they were with us. I think Adrian was okay with this for a while because it kept Cara busy and out of his hair, and mine, too, to be honest.

One day, the Department of Social Services showed up at my uncle and aunt's house and took all four of their children because of the condition of the house. They were going to be placed in a foster home if no family member would take them in. I was called and was told that the parents were being given six months to complete their classes, complete repairs, and get their children back. I was told that I would get assistance because I was going from one child to five children. It was two teenagers and two others around Cara's age. I explained the situation to Adrian, and he agreed hesitantly, saying that it would only be for six months and that DSS would help us with them.

It didn't take long to realize my uncle and aunt had no plans to get their children. Instead, they had responsible adults caring for them, and they found themselves able to go and do as they pleased. Soon, the phone call came saying they had not completed any of their classes or completed any repairs needed to close the case out and retrieve their children. The case worker asked if they had been coming by to visit the children. I told them they did for about a month but hadn't seen or heard from them since. My husband was not happy.

"What are we going to do?" He asked. "We cannot afford to take care of all these children on our own. Cara is our responsibility, and I'm not going to take care of someone else's child while their parents run around having a good time." He was right; six months had turned into three years, but what was I going to do? They were my cousins, but I loved them like they were my very own children.

I began to cry because I didn't know what to do. While this was going on, I felt as though I might be pregnant. I was late on my cycle and simply didn't feel well. I was throwing up every morning and feeling very sluggish.

I said, "Adrian, I think I might be pregnant."

He made a doctor's appointment. Oh my God, he was so happy. It felt like my marriage was finally going to turn around. The only problem was what were we going to do with all the other children? Unfortunately, before I could get to the doctor, my cycle came on. Both Adrian and I were devastated.

He said, "You embarrassed me to my friends because I told them that we were having a baby."

I felt worthless because I was sure. I knew it.

I explained, "I must have lost it."

He didn't believe me. I didn't bother going to the doctor because he didn't believe me anyway. I quickly got back into my routine, burying the hurt and anger I felt. My voice didn't matter. That seemed to enrage me more than anything we had gone through.

I prayed, "Lord, Why am I in this mess? God, you said that it was better to marry than to burn. I married him because we both needed someone. I wanted to do right before you, God. I'm not perfect, but, Lord, I've been faithful to him. I don't know how to be what he needs anymore. I just don't. Help me, Jesus!"

God doesn't respond!

The headaches started, and soon after, panic attacks. I tried my best to function, but I was stressed. I didn't know whether I was coming or going at times. I focused on the task before me and pushed my issues as far away as I could. When the blurry vision started, I went in to see my doctor.

He said, "Your blood pressure is extremely high, and you need to make some immediate changes to your life if you want to still be here."

My weight had also increased greatly because I stress ate.

I explained, "I would start trying to walk when I can, but honestly, I need to work because of the situation."

He stressed the seriousness of my situation and increased my blood pressure medication. He also added medication that would make me rest when I went to sleep.

We were able to hold on to the children for about 2.5 years before things got bad. My uncle and aunt refused to pay child support, and DSS cut off all benefits because they were my family, and my marriage was holding on by a thread. I began working two full-time jobs while my husband worked one. He worked long hours in the heat; therefore, he watched the kids after he got off.

One day, he said, "We need to talk!"

I knew where this was going.

He said, "You have done all you can for them, but now we all are about to be homeless. We have got to get rid of these kids. It's just too many of them. Someone besides us can take them."

I looked at them like they were my own babies; I just didn't know how to let them go. Adrian knew I was trying to do what was right in the eyes of God.

He added, "I am the head of the house, and I've made the decision."

My heart broke! With tears running down my face, I agreed and began to look for another family member to take them. Adrian got a second job to help get us out of the hole, and the kids stayed with my mom until we got off.

After about two weeks, I found an aunt on their mother's side who said she would get them to keep them from going into custody. On the day they were supposed to move, my daughter begged and pleaded that we not give them away. We explained that we had done all we could and were on the verge of losing our home and that my first responsibility was to her.

Cara said, "I would sacrifice everything as long as my sisters can stay with me."

With tears in my eyes, I told her, "They will still be with family and will come and visit as much as they want."

When we got to their aunt's house, she was not home. We called and called, but no answer. I contacted their caseworker, who informed us that she had changed her mind and that if we couldn't keep the kids, they would have to go into custody. I talked to Adrian, praying that God would intervene and he would have a change of mind.

He said, "I do not care even if they had to live in a box on the street."

I knew that day my marriage was over, and I didn't even try anymore.

Adrian went to work every day, and so did I. Though my cousins were gone, I continued to work two jobs, and

Adrian took care of Cara in the evenings. I would come home long enough to make sure there was food for them to eat for dinner, and I would be off to my night job. I was trying to prepare for what I knew was coming next. I want to make this clear, I still loved my husband but had lost all respect for him. I couldn't understand the comment he made. They were just babies; they were my own flesh and blood, and he would rather them be in a box on the street than with us. I rocked the little ones to sleep when they cried about missing their mom and dad. I kissed them and hugged them. To me, they were my children.

My mind went back to a day that I was off from work. I remember being so exhausted. The house was quiet, and I finally had time to sleep. As I walked from one room of the apartment past the bedrooms, the dirty clothes were piled high in every room. I decided the rest had to wait. I gathered all the clothes and headed to the laundromat.

My mom called as I was walking out the door. I answered the phone and said, "I will call you back as soon as I can because I'm headed to the laundromat."

She said, "Okay!"

By the time I got all the clothes in the washing machine, she walked through the door and said, "Need some help?"

I crumbled as the tears rolled down my face. I needed her in that moment. When all the clothes were dried and folded, we had approximately 50 pairs of pants, 50 shirts, 50 pairs of underwear, 50 pairs of socks, washcloths, towels, and other miscellaneous items. “All these clothes accumulated in one week, mama.” I hugged and thanked my mom and went home to separate the clothes into 7 piles so that everyone could put their clothes up. I remember thinking, “I’m too tired to cook; sandwiches it is,” and I went to bed. Our relationship was beginning to change, at least a little. I believe she knew I was doing all I could to make the situation work.

At this point, I couldn’t stand being around Adrian anymore, so I worked. I spent more time at my jobs than at home. When I wasn’t working, I was crying and worrying about my cousins.

After a few weeks, my mom called and said, “I saw how worried you were about the kids and decided to take them out of DSS custody.”

As soon as I saw her, I hugged and kissed her.

I told my mom, “I will help you in any way I can.”

My daughter finally had her sister’s back, and I could finally rest knowing that they would be safe. Cara decided she wanted to go live with her sisters at my mom’s house because she had no one to play with at our house. I finally gave in. Maybe this would relieve some more of the stress in the house because it wasn’t good for us or Cara.

That was one issue down, but my marriage was still in shambles. I started communicating with someone on my job who was sympathetic to what I was going through. I grew closer to him than I was to my own husband. He wanted to talk, and he took the time to listen when my husband thought I was crazy and a liar. Things with my husband was hard, but things with Warren was easy. Not to mention, he was ex-military, looked and smelled good, and had a great sense of humor. We became good friends, and I began to think less and less about Adrian.

Adrian came home one night that I was off and said, "We need to talk."

He realized that things had not been good between us.

He said, "I know that we have been on a roller coaster of wanting to be married today and tomorrow, not be. However, you are my wife, and the Bible says that it's your responsibility to have sex with me." He continued, "It has been over a month, and I need it!"

I said, "Really?"

He said, "Yes!"

I rolled over and said, "Hurry up."

When he finished, I rolled back over and went to sleep. I remember thinking, a*nother chore that I can check off my to-do list.*

In all honesty, I was numb from everything that was going on, but I did look at it like a chore because I was his wife, and it was a part of my responsibility. I was in it physically, but emotionally, I had checked out. Somewhere deep inside me, I knew I loved him, but in that moment, I simply didn't like him. I needed to check off yet another thing to do. He understood what I wanted and what was important to me. That's why he went there. Everything that I did was to try and please God, and if I had to suffer, so be it. The problem was I just didn't know enough about the God I was trying to serve.

I believe that we have to have head and heart knowledge, which will balance us. My heart was to serve Him, but I didn't have the knowledge to know how to go about it. It frustrated me because nothing was working, and I was serving God to the best of my ability.

It wasn't long before I started throwing up again. My cycle was late, and I started feeling tired all the time. It was hard to keep up with my two jobs, but I needed them.

One morning, he heard me throwing up and asked me, "What's wrong?"

I said, "I'm late and just don't feel good, and I'm tired all the time now."

He asked, "Are you pregnant?"

I replied, "I think so, but I'm going to make a doctor's appointment."

His face lit up with excitement, and he said, "Okay!"

Adrian left and went on to work, leaving me home in bed to rest. At about 12:30 pm, I felt well enough to get ready for my afternoon job. I made my doctor's appointment a month later so that I would be far enough along for the doctors to pick it up. However, one night, while in bed, I awoke to severe cramps, and I was bleeding. I quietly went into the bathroom and cleaned myself up, padding to ensure I didn't mess the bed up. I laid down and cried myself back to sleep. I didn't want to see that look in his eyes this time. The next morning, I got up and went to work. In my mind, I knew that I had to deal with it, but it was simply not going to be that day.

Adrian noticed that the throwing up had stopped, and I was acting normal.

He said, "So I guess you're not pregnant."

I said, "No, my period came on last week."

He said, "Ooooook."

I turned around and went to work. To be honest, I didn't know what to tell him. I didn't know whether it was my period or a miscarriage. All I knew was that I didn't ever want him to look at me the way he did before.

Cara stayed with my mother most of the time because we were working so much and, honestly, because she had access to some of her cousins. My mom stayed in a central area where some of the family lived within walking distance of each other. This allowed her to be around family versus being with us by herself. However, just as before, my mom would let me know what she needed, and I made sure she had it. In between shifts or on my days off, I would go get the girls and take them out to eat or do something they wanted to do. Cara was happy, and I was happy that she didn't have to experience all the stress Adrian and I were dealing with.

I eventually left Burger King and the Meps and started working driving a school bus full-time and a gas station part-time. This gave me benefits and flexibility during the day to help my mom out with doctors' appointments or run to the school to check on the kids. I loved going to my first job. I worked with some of the best people. We laughed and had each other's back on those buses. Even the supervisors were cool, and working with my friend Warren made it better. Before you get ahead of yourselves, no, I had not slept with this man. He was eye candy. I guess you can say he was a fantasy.

I'm not sure when or how it happened, but a few of us on the job went out to a club. Now, it had been approximately three years since I went out to a club. I really didn't want to go, but my coworkers knew I had been dealing with issues at home and felt a night out on the town could give me a break from the drama. I showed up to that club with a church dress on and church shoes. Oh, how they laughed at me. However, they just wanted me to have a good time unwinding and to take my mind off everything that was going on. I danced and laughed that night like I was once again a woman with no responsibilities.

Afterward, Warren and I ended up at his house, and let's just say my fantasy became a partial reality. I mean, we did everything except the actual act of having sex. I caught myself and decided to go home. As I lay beside my husband, I got so hot and bothered thinking about Warren that I woke him up already on top. That was a good night. Lord, that was a good night.

Approximately six weeks later, the throwing up started again, and my cycle was late. I didn't say anything to Adrian this time. I went in to see the doctor, and the urine test was negative. They said they wanted to take blood work to try to find out what was going on with me. They were thinking I had hormonal issues. They said they would call as soon as the results came in. I left and went on to work.

The results came in within two days. I was pregnant! I was shocked because this time, I hadn't built up my hopes because of the other disappointments. I had medical proof for Adrian. When I called him, I told him that the doctor just called and said we were having a baby. He was ecstatic. I thought, "God, is this really happening?" I made a promise to myself that I would do everything I could to make my marriage work for the sake of our baby. After all these years, God had finally blessed us. I called off from my part-time job to be with my husband. I felt, for the first time, we had a real chance of making it. This baby was going to change everything.

Within a week of finding out, my mother showed up at my job to tell me that one of my cousins had died. I immediately got lightheaded and started to pass out. My mother yelled and immediately grabbed me. My supervisor told me to go home because I couldn't work like that. I immediately started bleeding and cramping, and just like that, my baby was gone. I was unable to attend my cousin's funeral because of the miscarriage, so I kept my aunt's house open until the rest of the family returned. I was mourning three deaths all at once, My cousin, my baby, and my marriage. Everything in me knew that we couldn't make it through another blow of this magnitude.

After the bleeding stopped, Adrian took me to my follow-up appointment. The doctor did a thorough pelvic exam to try to determine what happened. He called Adrian back into the room.

The doctor said, "We've found evidence of multiple pregnancies or that you were pregnant with twins more than once. There is too much tissue to be one pregnancy. The times you thought you were pregnant, you were, but you were losing them before we could confirm them."

I asked, "Why wasn't I able to hold my babies?"

The doctor replied, "Stress."

I looked at Adrian with tears rolling down my face, and he dropped his head.

The doctor continued, "Can we run a test to determine if they were twins or separate multiple births?"

I said, "No, I don't want to know; this is painful enough."

They conducted the D&C, and we went home quietly.

I believe that we really tried to make things work, but it felt as though the deck had been stacked against us. So, we got back into the regular flow of things. I spent time with the kids and then went back to work, and he did whatever it was he was doing at that time. My days and nights became a blur. I believe Adrian was hurting just as much as I was, but it was just hard to continue as we were.

One day, while at work, Warren said he wanted a part-time job, so I told him I would get him a job where I was working, which was a convenience store. He was on the schedule within a couple of days, and Adrian was none the wiser. One day, while working, we decided that we wanted to finish what we started. It seemed curiosity had gotten the best of both of us. So, we made plans to meet.

I convinced myself that I was justified because my husband didn't love me, or at least that's how he acted. Both of us had suffered a loss, and it was hard, and I was tired of pretending. We had accomplished a lot of things together, but the one thing I knew he wanted God wasn't giving to us. I'm sure you can imagine how much we played the blame game. I was tired of hearing my own voice say the same thing repeatedly. So, I planned.

Warren and I finally hooked up. I really can't say how good it was because I was so nervous. In my heart, I knew I had betrayed my husband and sinned against God. For me, it was going to be a means to an end. When I got home that night, I immediately went and got in the shower. In my heart, I knew I had sunken to a new low. I got out of the shower and waited for him to go in for his bath.

I sat on the commode and said, "We need to talk."

He said, "About what?"

I said, "Do you ever remember telling me that if I cheated, you would leave and never come back?

He said, "Yes!"

I said, "Well, I did. Are you going to leave?"

He yelled, "What?"

He hit the water, and it splashed all over me and the floor. As he slowly rose out of the water, the anger on his face was obvious, and I began to laugh. Not intentionally, but it felt good because I felt as though he had been hurting me throughout most of our marriage, and now, he was feeling some of what I was. His pain seemed to strengthen me. You see, Adrian seemed too emotionless throughout our marriage. I secretly wondered if he even had a heart. This was the first sign of one that I had seen in years. Adrian took some time for himself to keep things from escalating, and I respected that. After he calmed down, he asked me specific questions about who the man was, where I met him, if I loved him, and if I was going to see him again. I answered honestly with a no, and we went to sleep.

Warren's purpose had been fulfilled, and I found another better-paying job. We never spoke again until some years later when he needed me to return the favor. I declined, and we haven't spoken since.

Adrian, on the other hand, refused to leave. I don't know what was keeping him there, but I could sense his hurt from my betraying him. Looking back, it was a dumb thing to do, but at the time, it was my only option, at least, that's the way it looked, or that's what I told myself.

We were married in every sense of the word but remained unhappy. One day, while he was watching the game, I became irritated and wanted him to go to my mother's house with me. We never did anything together.

He said, "No, I'm watching the game!"

I said, "Okay."

I went into the room, made a phone call to a girlfriend of mine, and packed some clothes for me and Cara. I left that day. It took almost 11 years for me to leave. There was no argument, no anything. It was just an urgency to get out of that situation. I simply couldn't take it another day.

I went back to the house once to discuss with him how we were going to handle everything as far as the furniture and paying our bills, seeing how we had been married for 11 years.

He said, "I'm not helping you with anything."

I left it alone and said, "We will talk later."

When I called, I could tell that something was different about him. He said he had a girlfriend, and I was cool with that until he started telling me what his girlfriend was saying about me and how he should handle me. I took Cara to school like I always did. I left and went straight to his job and told them I needed to see him ASAP. When he came out, I told him I needed to talk to him face-to-face about how to handle everything. We winded up going back to my girlfriend's apartment to talk.

He repeatedly said, "I need to get back to work."

I replied, "I'm tired of arguing, and the sooner we settle everything, the better."

He went to tell me what his girlfriend said.

I cut him off and said, "Please, don't make me strangle her with her own legs. All she knows is what you tell her."

He said, "Please, let's not get violent. I just don't have the money to pay any other bills."

The conversation went downhill at this point. There was no understanding and no reasoning.

I pulled out a knife and said, "You are going to be with your mother today."

He said, "My mother is dead."

I said, "Exactly. I really tried to make the marriage work, and yes, I was wrong for what I did, but you were wrong too."

You see, he didn't know I knew about the pictures of him and his friends in a motel room during bike week with women. One of his friends was crazy enough to take pictures, and his wife found them. I never told him. I was tired! As my hand went up in the air, my girlfriend walked through the door and caught my hand.

She said to him, "Go get in my car and lock the door."

She said to me, "Girl, you got a wild look on your face. I wouldn't have recognized you if I didn't know you."

After they left, I went to his job, slashed his tires, and keyed the entire car. I went to break the windows, but someone came out of the building. I left and went home and started to cry! I was no longer mad; I was in a state of rage. I called my job and told the director what had happened. He got me into emergency counseling, and I was placed on administrative leave with pay. I was told to report back to him when the doctor felt it was okay for me to return, and he would have me added back to the schedule.

I remember Adrian calling and saying, "My supervisor wanted to have you arrested."

I told him, "You should have so when I got out on bond, I could've come and stood across the street and blown your fucking head off. "

The line went quiet, and I hung up.

It took me a complete year for me to finally be able to mentally recover. God also allowed me to pay every bill off in a year. By the time the divorce papers came, I was able to sign them and put them back in the mail the same day. I never went to court. Today, he visits my mother and uncle whenever he wants to. I have seen him there on occasion, and we talk like nothing ever happened.

Cara and the two younger cousins grew up and eventually saw Adrian out working. They stopped to talk with him. When it was all said and done, he apologized to them all and hugged them. They said they forgave him. Cara is still close to him today.

Oh my God, it's really storming outside. I think I'm going to lie down and rest my mind and body until the storm ceases. It wasn't long before I fell asleep that Trevor entered my mind. We dated for about five to six years off and on. He was the kind of person that you would keep in contact with after the relationship was over. Trevor was about seven years younger than me. He was 29, and I was 36. He was black as two Ace a spade, and short. He wasn't much to look at, but he was the sweetest man I knew. I met him while working at the Department of Juvenile Justice. We became such good friends. Trevor was my go-to when life became too stressful. I remember the day we crossed the line, moving from friendship to relationship by sleeping together. I was tired of crying and hurting over a failed marriage. I had moved out, bouncing from place to place, trying to keep a roof over my daughter's head. This place was nice compared to the hotel we'd lived in for the past year. The day it happened, I reached up to him with tears in my eyes and kissed him. He pushed me away and said, "Do you know what you're doing?"

I said, "Yes, I'm tired of hurting, and even if it's just for tonight, I want to feel better."

I had never in my life experienced how this man made me feel. As I think back, it's not what's on the outside that matters. I had the Coca-cola shape and a pretty face but, deep down, I was torn up from the floor up. Here, this man, a man I didn't find physically attractive, was healing to my body and mind, if only for a season. He was everything I needed in that moment. He did it for as long as I needed, how I needed it, and as many times as I needed it. He touched my heart, and I touched his in ways neither one of us could have ever imagined.

However, Cancer separated us. He was diagnosed with the same type of cancer he had some years earlier. He was afraid to place his trust in anyone to be there for him. You see, he vowed he would never put me through what he and his ex-girlfriend went through. He said his first girlfriend was unable to handle it and left him right after he had open heart surgery. It devastated him. He struggled to find the strength to go on, but he made it by the grace of God. I had absolutely no doubt in my mind how much Trevor loved me. We became what each needed to get through the rough days that were approaching us both. He said without me, it would become unbearable. I felt the same.

One day, while we were making love, I heard someone say, "The wages of sin is death."

I said, "What did you say?"

Trevor said, "I didn't say anything."

I heard it again, "The wages of sin is death."

I realized it was God speaking to me. So, I sat on the side of the bed, and Trevor and I began to talk. He knew that I was a Christian, and to be honest, he was too. However, we both forgot about it because of our situations. What both of us were experiencing felt real and in our minds, we reasoned how could it possibly be wrong.

Trevor took a deep breath and said, "I want to be clear. I love you and would die to be with you. On my worst day, being with you is like sitting on a sunny beach en-joying life. I vow that once this cancer Is gone, you will be my wife and that we will spend the rest of our lives together, loving each other." He asked, "Can you wait for me?"

We kissed and fell back into each other's arms. Shortly after, I fell asleep. I dreamed of walking into a church where people were waiting for a funeral to start. People were standing around crying and talking. I walked up to the casket to see him lying there. Trevor was dead.

I woke up and turned to him, and he said, "Tell me what you saw."

With tears running down my face, I said, "I saw you dead! I was at your funeral in the dream!"

A strange look came over his face. Maybe he realized that what God spoke to me was bound to happen if we didn't stop. He got up, put on his clothes, and I walked him to the door. There was no goodbye, just a kiss that let me know I would never see him again. Our paths crossed over the years in the form of just checking in on each other through Facebook. After a while, they stopped, and I learned some years later that he had died. My heart broke.

I wonder why my mind went to him. Probably because this would be the kind of night that he would hold me tight until we fell asleep. Wow, it's still storming. When I was afraid, he was always there to comfort me and I him. My heart still aches for him; he was my friend through it all, and he still is. The world has lost a truly remarkable man. I had never heard him complain about what he went through. He put his best foot forward to be a better man than he was yesterday. He was an angel that was destined to return to glory. We never got our Happily Ever After. I found out years later that he was married the whole time. I didn't see that one coming.

Reflection

Looking back, I developed an I-can-fix-it mentality concerning the people in my life. It started all because I needed help and wanted to be the help that never came for me. Adrian, my uncle, my aunt, my cousins, and even Trevor became my projects. Because of my trauma early in life, I was now trying to save everyone and losing myself. Helping people is not wrong; however, my motive was. Helping them was not going to heal me; they needed Jesus, and I did too. So, my question to you today is, what are you doing that is a direct result of your trauma?

CHAPTER FOUR

The Fourth Hour: And so, the Training Begins

I remember sitting on the side of the bed one night, and the storm outside was bad. The thunder was loud and frightening, to be honest. I looked over, and my husband was no longer there. There was no one there to comfort me. I couldn't believe all that I had gone through in the past years of my life. I knew about prayer and had even attempted to do it every now and again, but I was exhausted, confused, and disappointed. I could feel that my life was supposed to be better, but it seemed I was sinking deeper and deeper into the hole that had become my life.

I whispered sobbingly, "God, what are you doing? I've only been on this earth for 35 years. I've been molested at 6, raped at 18, married at 23, had 3 miscarriages, now divorced at 35, and the one thing that I have tried my best to be is a mom. I wanted to be a mom to my daughter, but the very thing I wanted is the one thing I can't be right now because I have to work to get out of this hole. This was the beginning of my problems with Adrian. I fought to keep Cara with me, and now she's gone anyway. I'm still a part-time mother. I created this mess. And on top of all of that, I have 11 years' worth of bills to pay because Adrian won't help. I'm now 250 lbs. and on medication for high blood pressure, diabetes, cholesterol, and panic attacks. Lord, help me. Please, help me!"

I laid down and listened to the rain as it was hitting the pavement outside my window. The tears had soaked my pillow, and the side of my face was stained with my tears.

God spoke softly, "I've been with you the entire time. Remember when you were a little girl, and I allowed you to touch the smoke, and it stopped in midair as long as your finger was on it? And what about the time you and Adrian were on the verge of losing the jeep, and you prayed and asked me for the money, and as you were driving on your bus route, you saw all the money blowing in the air? I never left you, and I never will. Everything will be alright!"

My tears dried up, and I fell asleep.

***

The next few years were hard. As I stated in the previous chapter, I found a new job. I was working in the county jail. This job was a Godsend because it enabled me to work as much as I wanted. This is how I was able to pay off eleven years of debt in one year. My paycheck was twelve hundred dollars every two weeks. This was a dangerous job. We worked 12.5-hour shifts, and if we were short, that was a mandatory 16-hour shift, and we had to be back on time for our next scheduled shift.

I remember one day while working, we had received inmates from the mental health facility because they were closing them down in the city I was in. It was right after we changed shifts, and the other officer left. I let the medical team pass out medication, and I started to do roll call.

A detainee woke up and yelled, "All y'all ladies ain't nothing but mother fucking dick suckers."

"Quiet down," I said.

He got even louder and, this time, began to approach me.

"Quiet down and return to your bunk," I said.

He said boldly, "Fuck you!"

Then immediately tried to slap me. I leaned back, but the tips of his fingers hit my face. I hit him as hard as I could. He fell to the floor. I ran to him to finish beating the hell out of him. I became so enraged that I wanted to beat him for everything I had ever gone through. However, the nurse grabbed me and pinned me up against the wall. I called a code red, and the responding officers and supervisor entered the unit to see the detainee on the floor.

My supervisor asked, "What happened?"

Another detainee said, "He tried to hit her, but before we could grab him, she knocked the hell out of him. That's why he's on the floor with his shoes off. They were on when he went over there."

My supervisor had me leave the dorm to write my report.

In the office, he asked me, "What were you going to do before the nurse caught you. She said you pulled your radio."

I said, "Yes, I was going to keep beating him with that radio until he stopped moving or until you guys came in. I am a woman working in a dorm of sixty-five male detainees. I was going to protect myself at all costs!"

He laughed, and I went back to writing. After that, the jail became my training ground. You see, I was working with people who needed Jesus. I started singing in the dorms, and it seemed to calm the detainees. People were being fired for what God was covering me for. My supervisors told me that they knew what I was doing, but it kept the units calm, and they knew wherever I was, that would be one unit they didn't have to worry about. So, as they had their church services, I sang. God was doing something in them and in me. I don't think I realized it then, but looking back, I do now.

Now, God had given me a job, but I still needed a place. As I stated, I started out living with my girlfriend, who stopped me from hurting Adrian for some reason, but that didn't work long because she needed her own space. She was dating, and I was a third wheel with a child.

I ended up moving back to my mom's house, paying her $500 a month. I no longer had to worry about Cara because she was back with her cousins, and they were in middle school at this point. I wasn't around a whole lot, but she was being taken care of.

However, every night that I came home, Cara began to tell me about what was going on while I was gone during the day. She said her cousins would pick on her and that her grandmother would take their sides. It got so bad that one night, she called my job, crying hysterically on the phone.

Cara said, "I'm tired of being mistreated. I'm not going into the house until you come home."

I knew something was wrong because these were the same girls that Cara would have sacrificed everything for them to keep them close to her. They were her sisters.

That night, when I came home, I found Cara sitting out by the mailbox waiting for me. When I went into the house to find out what was going on, everybody said Cara was the problem. I took a deep breath, called a friend, and started to pack our things. We were there for maybe six months, top. I told my mom that I was tired of the arguing and that for the sake of peace, I was moving Cara and me in with a friend until I found someplace.

I ended up moving us in with a friend in another city, Sumter. This meant I had to move Cara's school as well. Once we were settled, we talked, and I started paying her and her husband $500 a month. There were three other children in the house, so Cara didn't feel alone. My girlfriend and I drove to work together and shared the responsibilities around the house. I thought everything was fine until the day she came in and accused me of sleeping with her husband. I could not believe it. I had only been there three months.

Her husband stepped up and said, "You're wrong. This woman and I have never even had a conversation in private, and you accuse her of this foolishness!"

I asked her, "Why did you ask me to come here if you figured I was that type of woman?"

I started packing and overheard her and her husband. He said, "Just because we cheated on each other in the past doesn't mean anyone's cheating now. She was your friend. She cooked, cleaned, and helped buy groceries, not to mention paying us $500 a month. You are wrong; you don't do a friend like this. You should have never brought her here if this was going to be how you acted."

Cara and I walked out the door, unsure of where we were going to go. I was tired of living with other people and it not working out. I found myself back in my hometown. Cara was almost asleep, so I pulled into an Intown Suites, paid the bill up to my next pay date, and told Cara to get ready for bed. I then finished unloading the car, and I fell asleep once again on a soaked pillow.

The Intown Suites was two hundred dollars a week. My hours were long, and I couldn't get off to pay the bill on time, so my mom agreed to pay it for me if I got it to her. It wasn't the best place, but it had two beds, a small refrigerator, a stovetop, a microwave, and cable. I allowed Cara to decorate it so it would feel more like home because it was for an entire year. Cara was able to walk to school because it was only a block away. She found friends because there were other children living there as well. I had to leave home early, so I talked to her about safety, and she did great. My baby was smiling again, though I felt horrible on the inside. One day, my mom came over to bring my receipts from paying the bill, and I was crying.

She asked, "What's wrong?"

I replied, "My life is terrible. I'm homeless, and I never thought that would be."

She said, "Ann, you're not homeless. Have you thought about how much you pay to stay here? You're paying eight hundred dollars, and you and Cara aren't living outside. You're doing a great job! Cara is not on Medicaid. You don't receive food stamps, and you have a roof over your head and a car to drive to a job that pays for all of it. Things will get better!"

I sucked it up and stayed focused on what I needed to do. On the thirteenth month, I moved into my own two-bedroom duplex, paying six hundred and fifty dollars a month. It was not far from Cara's school, that way she wouldn't have to move again. I moved my furniture out of storage and set up our new home. Cara was so happy because she had her own room once again. I could finally exhale! As I lay in bed that night, I thanked God, finally feeling like I had accomplished something, and drifted off to sleep.

I was so happy because Cara now had a place she could bring her friends that was safe and clean. She had also become very responsible because she knew that I was working. When I came home, Cara would have cooked and cleaned. I told her that I didn't mind if her girlfriends came to hang out or even spend the night as long as they weren't in my room. Sometimes, there would be so many kids sleeping on the floor that I would have to step over them to get to my room. I didn't care because, for the first time in a long time, we were happy.

After about two years, I heard the Lord say, "I'm moving you back home with your mother because she's getting ready to go through something, and she's going to need you. Give away everything that you have in this apartment. Don't sell it; give it away."

I said, "Lord, I have nice things, and I can put them back in storage."

He said, "No, give it away. I have someone I want you to give it to."

I got up and asked, "Who do you want me to give the furniture to?"

He said, "The young lady to the right of you."

I went and knocked on her door; the apartment was empty. She had 4 children, and all of them were sleeping on the floor.

I told her, "God led me to give away everything in my apartment."

She said, "I can't afford to pay you."

I said, "No, God told me to give it to you."

The next day, she received a living room set, 2-bedroom sets, 3 televisions, a washer and dryer set, and all the pictures hanging on my walls. She was so grateful. I then explained to my landlord what was going on concerning my mother, and he allowed me to break the lease so Cara and I could move back home with my mom. Within a couple of weeks, my mom was diagnosed with an aggressive form of breast cancer.

The girls were in high school now and starting to give my mom some trouble. I was there to handle what needed to be handled. My mom came through her surgery well but went back to work too soon and pulled the drainage tube that was still in her breast. I had gone to work that day, and the girls were home with my mother. Cara noticed that my mom wasn't getting out of bed. She was sleeping longer and, when awake, complained that she was cold. She went to my aunt, who checked on her and mentioned my mom said she would be up soon.

Now, anyone who knows my mom knows that she's the early bird. She would get up at 6 in the morning, sponge off, get fully dressed, drink her coffee, eat her breakfast, take her medication, and be outside, sweeping the yard by 7 am. Then, get ready for work. This was not the woman that they were seeing lying in the bed.

My aunt went back to her house, which was only a few feet away. She told Cara to come back and get her if my mom didn't get up soon. Cara waited another few hours and then called me at work. She said that it was now 3 pm and Grandma was still in bed. I asked her to go to the room and place her hand on my mom's forehead to see if she felt hot. Cara did it with me on the phone. She said, "Yes, ma, she's hot." My mom said she was fine, but she was speaking sluggishly! I told Cara to go and get her aunt right now.

Aunt Bee came down and placed her hand on my mother's forehead and began to scream. She grabbed the phone and said, "OMG. Get here now!" I said, "I'm coming, but it's going to take a minute because I'm at the jail, and they have to get someone to relieve me. Call the ambulance. I immediately called my sister and told her she needed to get to Mama ASAP because I had to get relieved before I could come. I told her that I would meet them at the hospital."

The ambulance arrived at the house, and my mother was loaded and taken to the emergency room. My sister got there first, and I got there shortly after her. Once they got my mom stable, the doctor said if she had not gotten there within the next hour, my mother would be dead. If pride and all the things we had been through stopped me from listening to the voice of God, this story would be different now. My daughter saved my mother's life. It brings tears to my eyes just thinking about it. This incident is what changed my mind and heart concerning my mother. Before, I think we tolerated each other, but that day, I learned the value of a mother. My mother, as hard as she appeared to be, her life was fragile and could be over in a moment. I worked harder at understanding the woman who was and is my mother.

Reflection

Looking back, I realize that God used the very situations in which I needed deliverance to begin my healing process. I hated men, and he placed me at the jail that paid me enough money to get out of debt, yet I had to deal with men every single day. I went from hating them to ministering to them as best I could. It was usually through songs that God revealed His call to me. I had to even move back home to take care of my mother, who was going to go through health issues. I learned that my mom could be taken from me at any time, so I let everything go. I learned that you can't run away from your problems. Know that the people in your life are more important than any issue you may have with them. God will stand with you when confronting your demons, and you will be victorious. So, my question to you is, are you willing to confront your demons?

CHAPTER FIVE

The Fifth Hour: Sleeping with the Enemy

I lived with my mother for approximately two years. It was long enough for me to save money and clean up my credit. I could hardly believe it, but I was now holding the keys to my very own home. It was built in the 50s, but it was all new to me. It was a three-bedroom, den, living room fireplace, one bath, and kitchen. It had a nice-sized carport and a huge yard. The backyard was fenced in, and there were flower bushes everywhere. The entire yard was shaded with trees. In no time, the house was completely furnished. Cara loved it, and so did I. My life was finally looking up. The girls were at the house most of the time, which made Cara happy. She finally had the relationship she used to have with them. She had her sisters back! The house soon filled with laughter. Life was good, and I was grateful. Lord, I was so grateful.

Cara and her cousins/sisters were now teenagers and started to see their older sisters. Unexpectedly, one of the older girls had a baby that died in his sleep. The girls wanted to go over to her house, which was right around the corner. I dropped them off and noticed a tall, light-skinned man there who waved at us. Later, I found out he was Damien, the real father of the girl whose baby died. I didn't see him again until the day of the funeral. He was dressed rather shabbily, but that really didn't matter to me. I was in no position to judge anyone, especially given my past. After the funeral, I cooked and invited all of them over, a kind of repass. However, Damien didn't show up. I asked why, and his sister said he was shy because it wasn't too long since he got out of prison. I told her he was more than welcome to come. After all, he was family. She called him, but he still felt uncomfortable, so I went over to their house to talk to him. After a few minutes of persuading him, he finally decided to come, and we all had a great time that night.

Damien and I became inseparable. We talked a lot about what we wanted out of life, and he said that being locked up and away from his family made him want to live a better life. He went on to say he had been in and out of prison for half of his life, and he needed a change.

"How long had you been locked up?" I asked.

"About 25 years all together," he said.

Something deep within me knew there had to be more to the story for a man to be in and out of prison for 25 years. I have to admit it piqued my curiosity. In truth, Damien and I were a lot of like. We took different roads, but from what I could see, we were in the same place. A place called failure. I worked in the prison system, and he was an ex-inmate. I felt that I had failed in so many ways and most definitely had many regrets, and though I had the opportunity to be around my family, our relationship wasn't the best. I was also looking for a better life. Up until this point, my life sucked, and Damien became a great distraction from the train wreck that was my life. I thought less about my own issues and focused on helping him get established. Between working long hours at the jail, the kids, and Damien, my plate was now full. I thought less about what I didn't get right and focused on what I could.

I said to him, "I want to help you because I know what it was like to struggle with little to no help. We are always together anyway. What do you need to do?"

He said, "To find a job, get a stable address and have a stable phone."

I said, "Well, you can move here. The kids know you, and I like having you around."

He agreed. I added a couple of dollars to what he had, and we went to Goodwill to buy clothes so he could start looking for a job. Now, I want you to understand though I liked him, there was no sexual relationship between us. I think he unknowingly became my project.

After a couple of months, I came home from work to find the lights down low. He met me at the door and blindfolded me. He then walked me to my bedroom. Once there, he took off the blindfold.

"I wanted to do something special for you," he said.

The room was lit with candles, and flowers covered the floor. He grabbed my hand and led me down the hall, which was also covered with flower peddles. When I got to the bathroom, it was also lit with candles, scented oil, and soft music playing. He undressed me, and I got in the tub. He proceeded to bathe me. Once that was done, he led me back to the bedroom, where he dried me off and dressed me in my gown. He told me to wait there, and he brought me a steak, baked potato, and mixed vegetables with nonalcoholic wine. After eating, he took the dishes to the sink and returned to the room. He crawled into the bed, kissed me, and held me until I fell asleep. I couldn't believe it. I remember sighing in relief. He didn't try anything. The next morning, we talked about getting married.

***

I was attending service at a small church a little way away.

Damien asked, "Can I attend service with you?"

I said, "Sure."

I was becoming more and more impressed every day by his desire to truly change. He wasn't just talking but doing things to make the change a reality. He was looking more like the man of my dreams every day. He cooked, cleaned, and wanted to go to church, and though we were staying together, he never tried to sleep with me. I spoke deep within myself that this must be God. All he needed was a job, and this situation would have been perfect.

Damien joined the church the first day he went and then requested a meeting with the pastor.

He said to the pastor, "I'm not sure if we should get married because we haven't been knowing each other that long."

I was convinced it was God, so I had no reservations. The pastor asked a series of questions, and we answered honestly.

The pastor asked, "Do you love each other?"

We said, "Yes, we think so."

He added, "You already living together?"

We said, "Yes, but not sleeping together."

He said, "Are you eventually planning on getting married?"

We both nodded yes, "We are planning a wedding."

He said, "Then get married here in my office and have your wedding later. That way, you will be right in the eyes of God."

We came out one day the next week and got married before the next service. It was three weeks before we consummated our marriage. I couldn't figure out what the problem was.

I finally asked, "What's wrong?"

He said, "I've been suffering from bad diabetes, and it has affected me in that area."

I asked, "Why didn't you come to me about it?"

He said, "I was ashamed!"

I replied, "We just need to get you seen by the doctor."

He agreed, and I called and made an appointment. After getting on the proper medications, everything was fine.

Twenty-nine days after being married, Damien dropped me off to work one day and said, "I'm going to buy some mulch for the flower beds."

According to him, he went into the store, bought five bags of mulch, and stole the sixth bag. Now, I don't know why he did this because he knew there was over two thousand dollars in the glove compartment of the car from my tax refund. As he rounded a curve and headed home, the mulch shifted in the trunk and forced the car off the road down into the woods. Damien was thrown out of the car through the passenger side window, which was slammed against a tree.

Immediately after finding out, his sister called the jail to tell me the news. She said she was on the way to get me. It took a while to get relieved, but I headed to the hospital as soon as I could. When I got to the hospital, the doctor said that he was paralyzed and that they didn't know whether he would live or die.

I spent my thirty-day anniversary in the hospital, praying that my husband would survive. The days ahead were hard. However, I never thought I would have to deal with what was coming my way. I stayed off work for a little while but had to return, so I set up a snack station for those who were willing to sit with him while I worked. My mom stayed with him while I slept during the day. Then, I would sit with him until it was time to go to work. Sometimes, Cara would stay, and every now and again, his daughter would stay. The reality was that Damien was now a quadriplegic, and he needed constant care. I sat quietly, trying to process it all as I prayed, asking God to heal my husband.

One day, he said he needed to speak to me. He could barely talk, so I had to get close.

He said, "I tried to cheat on you with a man in our house. It happened one day while you were out working. But because of erectile dysfunction caused by the diabetes, I couldn't do it."

He continued, "The second thing was that I needed to get the change out of the trunk of the car."

I asked, "What change?"

He said, "While you were working, I was going around robbing laundromats that were abandoned."

I was speechless.

He said, "I tried, Ann. I really did try. I would get urges that overwhelmed me at times. It's like a crackhead feening for crack."

The tears began to roll down my face, and a pain deep within me began to rise. It was a feeling I had never experienced in my life. My husband was gay and a thief. I was humiliated in that moment. I didn't say anything to anyone to protect him, but I also did so because I was embarrassed. I needed to process what he said to me. All kinds of questions were running through my mind. I silently cried as he drifted off to sleep. I was blown away by his so-called deathbed confession. He wanted to clear his conscience just in case this was it.

My entire life had fallen apart again! I didn't know how to process the range of emotions I was experiencing. One moment, I was devastated because I didn't know whether he would live or die. He was my husband, and despite it all, I wanted what was best for him. I also felt that I was responsible for his accident because our lives were so different, and he simply wasn't prepared. I worked in law enforcement, and he was a crook. I was saved, and it's obvious now he wasn't. I gave him the benefit of the doubt. How could I not see the signs? I was a fool! A stupid fool. I thought that he really wanted something different out of his life, and I married this man. I wanted to give him a chance because I understood what it was like to have to build a new life out of nothing. I was mad, in fact. I was mad as hell. I should've never gone to his daughter's house that day. What was I going to do?

Damien also totaled the car, and I was now forced to get a ride back and forth to work. Thank God a Christian coworker of mine decided to help. My entire world had just been shot to hell, and I was stuck wondering, what have you done? If I am to be honest, I wasn't sure if I was wondering what in the world I had done or what he'd done. All I knew was my life had changed, and it was not for the better.

Finally, after a month, he was stable enough for them to start him on soft foods. I stood beside him, trying to be the best wife I could be despite everything he told me. I remember one of his sisters telling me to "Put him in a home; you guys haven't been married that long. We would understand!" I thought about the vows I made and decided to stay. I was fighting within myself. I knew that the marriage would never be the same, but he was a human being in a bad situation.

Damien started physical and occupational therapy. The better he got, the more bitter he got. He became nasty and vindictive. He would have me crying every day because everything in me wanted to leave, but I made vows to this man for better or worse in sickness and in health until death do us part. In truth, I hated him as much as I loved him. But I had given up and walked out on my last marriage, and this time, it wouldn't be me who gave up. I didn't care about what I had to go through. I just needed to win this round. Damien didn't make it easy. Now that he was able to talk, he had a lot to say, and none of it was good.

One day, while at the hospital, Damien started in on me, and my mom asked me to leave the room. When I returned, the room was weirdly quiet.

I asked, "Is everything alright?

My mother said, "Yes."

She later told me that she told him that he had a good wife, one that was paying bills, feeding the dogs, taking care of the kids, and now dealing with a sick husband while working a job 12.5 hours a day. She said, "You will not disrespect her another day in front of me because I will wet this towel and beat the hell out of you, and nobody will know."

After another month, it was time to prepare for him to go home, so every day for a week, I had to go and take classes on how to care for a quadriplegic. I had to learn how to bathe him to ensure his skin didn't break down. I had to give him two to three enemas a week, after which I had to clean him. The first few times, I would gag, which only enraged him. I had to feed him and do his hygiene, of course, the way he wanted things done. I had to do daily stretches, which would keep his muscles from getting tight. If not, he would be in extreme pain. I passed all their test. They also ordered his hospital bed and Hoyer lift and set up for him to receive medical supplies such as pull-ups or adult diapers, wipes, gloves, and bed chucks. They also fitted and ordered his electric wheelchair, which was all paid for by state Medicaid. He was also assigned a case worker from the Department of Special Needs. The doctor said she would come to do her assessment within a few days of him getting home. I put in for some time off when the day was set for him to go home. I sat down in a chair and took a deep breath.

Damien asked, "Are you sure you're going to be able to do this?"

I said, "I guess so."

The day came for his discharge, and an ambulance brought him home. There were no more nurses or doctors, just me. Cara had gone to college, and the other girls were out on their own by then. They placed him in the bed, and I made him as comfortable as I could. As soon as the drivers left, he wanted something to eat. He was placed on a low-carb, high-protein diet, which he hated. However, the doctor said he broke a bone in his neck and he already had medical issues, so the healthier he eats, the better he will be. After I finished feeding him, I cut the television on to his favorite show. I had to get the house ready for all of the medical stuff that was coming. The Hoyer lift came, and a folding wheelchair within hours.

I called his case worker to let her know he was home; she said, "I would be out first thing in the morning."

I was also sent home with a lot of different prescriptions, so I asked my mom if she would go and get them filled because he couldn't be left alone. Family began to show up to see him, and that made him feel a little better. Once the house was clear and my mom brought back his meds, I was ready to wind down; it had been a long day, and I just needed a minute. I gave him his medication, put him in a comfortable position, and laid down on the floor beside his bed. The doctor said he could stop breathing during the night; therefore, I needed to be close to hear his breathing patterns.

As Damien slept, the tears rolled down my face because I felt like I was over my head, and I honestly didn't know how I was going to handle it all. While I lay there, I listened to his breathing patterns, and when they became shallow, I would get up and check on him. He would be sound asleep. I was told that I needed to change his position every two to three hours to prevent sores. That would be impossible because I wouldn't get enough rest to sustain me. So, I told him to let me know when he needed to be moved. The medication made him sleep all night. Lord knows I was grateful for the rest because I was running for him and me during the day. I need to say this, I commend anyone taking care of a loved one. It's hard, and in my case, this was new to Damien and me. He had to adjust, and so did I. You see, Damien was used to doing things himself. However, now I had to do it for him. Instead of getting everything he needed at one time, he would ask one at a time.

Before I sat down, I started asking, "Is there anything else?

He would get angry.

I explained, "I am running for both of us now, and it's extremely tiring."

He took it as if he was being a burden.

I reassured him as his wife, saying, "We will get through this together."

The next morning, the caseworker came and explained the waiver to me.

She said, "Due to Damien's injury, he is placed at the top of the list, so he will be eligible for other benefits regular Medicaid doesn't pay for. You'll have medical power of attorney as his wife, and he's eligible to have a CNA come in to give you a break. He also qualifies for respite hours, and we will also put a ramp on the back side of the house and make the house more handicap assessable."

This was an answer to my prayers.

She continued, "I must be clear that at no point or time can your husband be left alone. You are now responsible for him, and he cannot be left alone for any reason. Not even to go outside to hang his clothes on the line."

I replied, "I understand. I need the home health service to start as soon as possible because I'll be returning to work soon."

She said, "I'll work on it."

My days ran into weeks quickly. I was constantly up, moving and doing. Damien was used to doing things his way, and he did not realize that I was now basically taking care of two people. If he had an itch, I was the one to scratch it. It seemed that as soon as I sat down, he was calling me to do something else. He just wasn't getting it.

I remember the first day that I had to give him an enema. All the supplies came but the gloves. I literally had to clean poop with no gloves. I thought I was going to throw up, but I knew he was embarrassed that I had to do it. So, I sucked it up and did what a wife was supposed to. You see, I learned that it wasn't just his ability to walk that had been taken away but his manhood as well. I'm going to be honest, I was struggling because no matter how sick he was, this man cheated on me, committed crimes, and caused his own accident. Not to mention that he was growing more and more bitter towards me every day. I was so exhausted mentally and physically; I was done and needed a break.

My aunt called and said, "Remember that you paid for your trip to the Bahamas for your honeymoon. You can't get your money back, so you guys should go."

I forgot about it during everything that had happened.

I replied, "But Damien can't do anything for himself, and I would need help with him."

She said, "We're family. Don't worry about that!"

I went to Damien, reminding him of the cruise, and he seemed to perk up.

"Damien, this isn't going to be easy, but if you really want to go, the rest of my family is willing to help us," I said.

He agreed excitingly. Now Damien was now a month back home and we were going on a cruise. We were leaving in a week, and I needed to start packing. I packed everything that I thought I might need. Finally, the day came.

My aunt rented a sixteen-passenger van, and we were ready to load up. Everyone got in the van except Damien, me, and two of my cousins. They lifted him in the van and pulled him up so he could sit straight up. I then got in to ensure he didn't fall over. They folded his wheelchair and placed it in the back, and we were off. This was a long ride because Damien had to lean on me for support to keep from falling over for about 12 hours. Though the road trip was long, it was welcomed because there was family, food, and fun!

Once we got to the terminal, my cousins assembled his chair and placed him back in it. Cara pushed Damien, and my cousin and I pushed the Hoyer lift and carried the suitcases. Once we made it to the entrance of the terminal, the porters took everything, and we were escorted all the way to the ticket desk. Once I presented our documents, we were escorted to the waiting room to await boarding.

My family caught up with us, and we were finally ready to board. We took pictures, laughing as if everything was going to be okay. I felt like both of us needed this trip because our lives were in shambles, and I needed to forget, even if only for a little while. Besides, Damien would never act crazy in front of my family. I wanted Damien to see that there was more in this life than what he had seen. He was used to a thugged-out life, and I was used to doing what was right.

After getting checked into our rooms, I wanted to know if he needed a break off his bottom. He said he wanted to go get something to eat. We all kind of went our separate ways from that point. Cara went with her cousins, who promised to come around when he needed to be moved from the chair or placed in the chair. Damien and I decided to enjoy all that we could; after all, it was supposed to be our honeymoon. He was limited and could only go into certain parts of the ship or ports because of the chair. However, we did and saw everything we could, especially eating, lol. I really wished he could have done more, but being on that ship was so relaxing. I knew I would be taking another one, as those three days went by so fast, and we were back in the van headed home.

It wasn't long before we were back home and had settled into our routine. The electric wheelchair had finally come, and the CNAs had started. It took a little while for me to train them in taking care of him specifically, but they were honestly a blessing.

Damien said, "He loved me, and he promised he would do better by not disrespecting me and trying to do some things on his own, like brushing his teeth and washing his face. He said he realized that our trip took a lot for me to pull off, and he was grateful to have gone. He said he realized that most women would have dumped him in a home and would have gone on with their lives. So, he wanted us to work on the marriage together."

I said okay, but deep within, I just didn't know how to come back from all that was said.

I was starting to have problems with my knees due to working on concrete floors in the jail, coupled with the weight I'd gain, not to mention the added tension from running for Damien as well.

My doctor asked, "What is your daily routine? I understand that your job is demanding. I suggest significant weight loss for you. I know you may do everything you can at home to reduce the stress off your knees. But weight loss would be your best avenue to reduce the pain. I can give you cortisone shots to help until you can lose enough weight to be of any significant help. However, you can only get a shot every three months."

I started going to get cortisone shots to deal with the pain. The shots worked well for the first month, and I was able to move on with a resemblance of what I considered to be a normal routine. Damien and I would get on the city bus and travel anywhere we wanted to go around the city. We went to the park, movies, malls, restaurants, etc. However, after the month, the pain would be unbearable, and I wouldn't be eligible for another shot for 2 months. The pain became unbearable, and I started to live off Motrin and Tylenol.

I was so happy when Damien was placed in the system for a handicapped transportation service. I no longer had to walk to catch the city bus. Instead, they came to our door and dropped us off at our destination. Lord knows this was a God-sent because my knees were taking a beating trying to be a normal couple. I wanted to make his life as normal as possible.

After a few months, Damien was finally able to balance himself in the wheelchair and operate it safely with great control. He was soon able to venture out of the yard and explore the neighborhood. He had gotten better with his hygiene. He was now brushing his teeth and washing his face. Life was finally moving in the right direction.

Damien said, "I want us to start going to church on your weekends off and hanging out."

I agreed and scheduled the handicapped van to pick us up the following Sunday.

We had a great time in church that Sunday, seeing how it had been so long since we had been there. The praise and worship were awesome, and the pastor preached a Word about God's love for us. We concluded with a nice dinner, and we both passed out in front of the television.

Days turned into weeks and weeks into years very quickly. Things appeared to be going well when we decided to have a cookout. Family and friends showed up. Damien invited a kid from around where his daughter lived. At this point, Damien was able to travel miles away from home as his wheelchair could get 26 miles on one charge. This kid seemed harmless. However, when it was time for him to go home, Damien said that he would walk him halfway.

I was kind of upset about it and told him, "I feel you need to stay with everyone else at the cookout."

He insisted, saying, "I want to make sure the boy got home safe."

Now, this was a teenage boy; I'm sure he could have found his way home. I mean, we were only a few streets over. Within about thirty minutes to an hour, Damien returned.

A few minutes after that, his daughter came running in and said the boy had told his parents that Damien molested him.

I felt as though the life was sucked out of me. She was literally screaming.

I said, "Please, explain what supposedly happened?"

She said, "They went up to the middle school, which is a block from our house, and Damien lured him behind the building, leaned forward and touched his penis."

I replied, "That didn't happen!"

She said, "Yes, it did! I know it happened!"

I said, "How do you know?"

She said, "Because he did it to me."

"What did you say?" I asked sincerely.

She said, "He used to have sex with me!"

I looked at him and walked away. I heard the two of them arguing.

I went back into the room and said, "Look, it is impossible for your father to lean over and touch someone's private because he is seat belted in the chair. He doesn't have the range of motion needed. His therapist and doctors could verify that."

I need you to understand I, too, had been molested, and no one protected me. There just was no physical way for Damien to do what they said.

So, I asked if the boy was sitting in Damien's lap?

She said no.

I said, "Then, no, it didn't happen." I didn't ask the question to defend my husband but to find out the facts. Deep within me, I just knew something wasn't right with this situation. I worked and lived with him every day, doing range of motion and working with him to help him gain strength and stability in his core. He simply didn't have the control or strength to do what was alleged.

Damien's daughter left the house.

I looked at Damien and asked, "What happened?"

Before he could answer, the child's parents were on the phone. I took a deep breath and answered. They explained to me what the child said happened.

I asked, "Was the child riding on Damien's lap?"

They replied, "No!"

I said, "Then it couldn't have happened because he simply did not have the range of motion necessary to do what he is being accused of. But do what you feel you must, and the truth will come out!"

This kid appeared to be around 13 or 14 years old. He was stronger and faster than Damien. He himself could have beat the hell out of Damien for trying something like that, or at the very least, have his parents come beat the hell out of him. Something just wasn't adding up!

After I got off the phone, Damien finally explained what happened.

Damien said, "The boy asked me if he could have my Walkman because it was a nice one. I said no, and the child got angry, went home, and told his parents this lie."

I asked, "How did you meet this child?"

He said, "His dad sold drugs in the neighborhood."

"What! Were you buying or selling?" I asked.

He looked at me, laughed, and rolled off.

I said, "Listen, if you are selling your prescription pain pills, I promise you won't have to worry who called the police, I would."

The rest of the night was quiet as I cleaned up and put Damien to bed. As I got ready for bed myself, I began to question what I was doing there. This day started out so nicely—our life was starting to settle down, and this cookout was supposed to be a celebration of what we made it through. Instead, Damien is accused of molesting a child, and his daughter confesses he also molested her. Lord, I'm at a loss for words. However, the first thing I need to do is deal with this current situation. I whispered, "Lord, let the truth come out; either way, let the truth be revealed." I then laid down, falling asleep to my own sobs.

***

My head was reeling, trying to process it all when the police showed up to arrest him the next day. Lord, it was the most humiliating process to go through as his wife. However, I knew that this simply couldn't have happened the way I heard it. They tried to force a 6'5 quadriplegic into the back of a police car. I told them if they hurt him, I would be suing. They finally gave up, put him back in his chair, and gave us instructions to report to court in two days. The looks of the police made me feel as though I was the one accused. I was outraged with Damien because I told him to stay home that day.

Because it was so soon, I couldn't get him scheduled on the handicapped van. So, we had to catch the city bus. With every step closer we got to the police station, I felt more and more sick in the stomach. We finally sat before the judge and the parents, who were laughing. The judge allowed the father to speak.

The boy's father said, "I feel so guilty because I thought Damien was a friend, and the fact that he would do something like this to my son is unthinkable."

The judge replied to the boy's parents, "It's not your fault. We, as parents, don't always know who we are letting our children around. However, that is what the courts are for to deal with this type of deviant behavior."

She turned to us and asked, "Do you have anything to say?"

I replied, “Damien could not have done what the child said because of his disability.”

The judge said, “I don’t want to hear you defend him.”

I said, “Ma’am, listen. I have never been in trouble with the law in my life. I have worked in the police system for almost ten years, and my husband knows that if I knew this to be the truth, there would be no way I would be standing here now. I thought the justice system was innocent until proven guilty; it doesn’t sound like that here to me. In the end, we will see who the deviants really are.”

She gave him a PR bond because there was no place in the jail to house a quadriplegic who was in total care. They also gave him a public defender and ordered him to stay away from all kids until the trial.

“Thank you for supporting me,” said Damien.

“If I believed you did this, I wouldn’t be here. But I have to tell you I’m mad as hell because I asked you not to go, and we haven’t even discussed the accusations of your daughter yet, and I am already mortified.

I felt me becoming overwhelmed by the stealing that led to his accident, the transvestite he tried to sleep with, the robbing of the laundromats, having to deal with allegations of him molesting another child, and having sex with his daughter, not to mention the possibility of him selling his prescription medication. The tears began to run down my face, and I could no longer contain myself. I was losing it, and I felt that my life was now some crazy movie on Lifetime. However, Damien rolled quietly beside me to the bus stop to head home.

The process ahead was long and degrading. I remember the day he needed to go in for questioning, and the investigator kept him back so long to where he had a bowel movement. She sprayed him with an air freshener, laughed, and said, "You can go now. He's crapped his pants." We had to get on the bus with him smelling like that. I was embarrassed for me, but I was also embarrassed for him. After being out all day, I had to come home, clean him up, and start dinner. He was mad because I left him in bed for the rest of what was left of the day. He wasn't happy, but I was too tired to care.

On top of this, we were now about two weeks from the court date. I decided to call the Public Defender's office, saying, "We have not heard anything from his public defender, and the case is in two weeks. "

They responded, "It doesn't take them long to prepare for a case." They will reach out soon!

I knew what that meant. I immediately began to pray.

"Lord, I wasn't there. I know in my heart that he didn't do this. However, I'm placing this in your hands, God. You be the judge and jury, and whatever the enemy has plotted and planned, God block it and bring the truth to light.

A week later, we received a letter saying that the case had been dropped because of a lack of evidence. They also said that the child constantly changed his story as if he had been coaxed into what to say. Tears streamed down my face, and I handed the paper to Damien.

He smiled and said, "Thank you for believing in me. Without you, I know I would have ended back up in prison." I said, "Damien, I did what any wife should, but it was God who vindicated you. The truth is many people go to jail because of their prior records. God never showed me you did this. You've done a lot but not this, and God answered my prayer by revealing the truth."

"Now that it is behind us, it's time to deal with the elephant in the room." Taking a deep breath, I said, "I want to know about the comment your daughter made."

"Yes, it's true. It happened when I had custody of her. She used to walk around naked to tempt me. I finally got tired of telling her no, and it happened," Damien said.

I was furious with him.

"So, are you saying it's her fault?"

He went to answer, and I screamed, "Shut up. She is your child. Your responsibility was to beat her ass and tell her to put some clothes on, not consent to having sex with your own child. Your own daughter knows more about you sexually than I do, and I'm your wife. This sickens me, and I need time to process this."

Everything in me wanted to leave, but I made a promise to myself that I wouldn't be the one to walk out this time. However, I honestly didn't know what to do. I myself had been molested. How could I possibly be attracted to and marry someone like this? How God? How?

I tried to stay busy, so I worked as much as I could, but I ended up on disability in 2009 because my knees finally went out. Our house became quiet because I honestly just didn't know what to say. So, we started going to a church right around the corner from us. It started at 1 pm, which gave the aide time to give him breakfast, bathe him, dress him, and get him in the chair. We felt so welcomed on the first day. To be honest, I looked forward to the services, and it took my mind off what was going on in my marriage.

By this time, I had purchased a van for us to get around in. One of my friends at the time was going through a great depression. I decided to drive to the beach to see her. While there, the place seemed so peaceful. I heard the Lord say move here.

I looked at Damien, and he said, "God told you to move here, didn't he?"

I said, "Yes, did you hear it?"

He said, "Yes."

I began to pray for confirmation.

That following Sunday, the pastor of the church said, "God told three couples to move. If it is you, please stand."

I was in shock. He went one by one, giving a specific word to each couple.

When he got to us, he said, "God is going to give you favor in the city you're moving to. God is going to increase your income almost 3 times what it is now once you get there. God is going to birth ministry through you there."

This was a hard move for me, so I procrastinated for another 3 to 6 months. I tried to get my house refinanced because I had gotten behind trying to take care of Damien. You see, he was placed on disability, and he received all the medical benefits but nothing monetarily. I was footing the bill for it all.

God said, "MOVE, and I will provide for you!"

It took a minute to pack up the entire house, but I finally got it ready. Now I had to find a place at the beach. God led me to an apartment about 6 miles from the beach. The area was beautiful and expensive. I wasn't sure if we'd meet the requirements.

God said, "Go inside."

Once inside, we were told that they were running a special for half the deposit and that only one of us needed to apply. However, both had to have background checks, and if there were no prior arrests, we would be good to go.

I explained, "Damien had a previous criminal record but nothing recent." Never mentioned the allegations because the charges were dropped, and besides, if it was going to be a problem, God wouldn't have sent me there, and two, it would've showed up on His background check, which they would have caught anyway.

They said, "We will run it and see what happens."

Damien's report came back clear first, and mine took forever. A phone call was made to find that my report was sitting on someone's desk. The lady on the other end of the phone said my record was clear and that she would walk the paperwork to the proper department and fax it immediately. I put the prorated deposit down, and we were given a move-in date. God worked out everything just as the pastor prophesied.

Looking back, I realized it was never really about Damien and me but God getting me in a position to use me in this new city to effect change for the kingdom of God. However, I had to be changed first. Damien was just a tool God used to bring about some of the change.

I remember that day well because it was the coldest day of the year, and God had worked a miracle right before our eyes. Damien and I talked about how it was downstairs, handicapped equipped, twelve hundred square feet, two bedrooms with a washer and dryer connection. The apartment was about the size of our entire house, and the property was beautiful, with a swimming pool, tennis court, weight room, and laundry room. It also had ponds, ducks, and palm trees throughout the property. Everything in me knew this was the hands of God. I immediately got nervous because reality set in that I was moving away from my family and friends to go to a place where I really didn't know anyone. Yes, I had a friend and her family there, but there was no blood of my own. God reminded me of his Word that he would give us a family that wasn't born of blood but by Spirit.

He said, "It will all work out, I promise."

It had been a long yet productive day, and I was ready to lay down and process the events of the day. I stopped to get us dinner on the way back to our hometown. By the time I pulled into the driveway, I was exhausted. I undressed Damien and sponged him off.

I said, "The aid will give you a bath in the morning." I cut on his TV, handed him his remote, and fell into bed myself. I don't remember getting undressed. I do remember hearing snoring, but I can't tell you whether it was mine or Damien's. The next thing I remember was looking out the window to see daylight peeking through the curtain. Damien was still sleeping when the aid began to knock on the door. Damien was too tired to get up, so she gave him a few hours and did small things around the house to finish getting ready for the move. I was grateful for the help. She wasn't like a lot of the other aides. She came to work, and she cared about her clients. I have had to fire so many of these ladies because they would get too close to Damien and not show up for their job, yet they wanted to get paid.

I remember this one girl who literally was flirting with my husband in front of me. She thought I was asleep, but the truth is I heard every word both said. They were planning what they were going to do once I went to work that day. I sat up and repeated word for word what I heard. They looked at each other and dropped their head.

I told the aide, "It would be in your best interest to leave my house and never come here again."

He explained there was nothing going on between us. I knew you wasn't asleep, but I just wanted to see what you would say or do."

I said, "Well, now you know!"

I called her employer and reported what happened, and they apologized and sent another aide. I found out this young lady continued to come to see him on the weekend while I was at work. She brought him food and whatever else. I'm not even sure if they slept together, but I eventually confronted them for the final time and contacted her agency. I never heard from or saw her again.

However, Monique wasn't like that. She was a professional, and the truth is I didn't know if I would ever find someone like her ever again. Though her job was coming to an end, she showed up every day and did what I needed her to for Damien. This freed me up to get all of Damien's services transferred to another county, such as setting a date for his bed to be picked up and another delivered to the new location.

My uncle and his friend agreed to drive the moving truck, and we were set to leave in less than a week. A friend of mine came by one day to talk to Damien and me.

She said, "God has given me a Word, and it's important that I tell you before you leave. Damien, God said it would be in your best interest to stay rather than go to another city with the same mindset. God is moving your wife for ministry, and He would not allow anyone to stop her from moving forward in it."

Damien nodded and said, "I understand, but I love my wife, and I thought that this would be a new beginning for us."

Now, I didn't know about ministry. I felt as though I had gone through too much and, to be honest, did too much to ever be used by God. I was reminded of the last ministry I was in and how God used me to chastise the pastor. The pastor appointed leadership that formed a prayer line. Instead of praying, the leadership would talk about the people running the members away from the church. God gave me a vision that the pastor was holding the door open while the wolves came in to devour the sheep. I had already left the church, so I wrote her a letter explaining what God had shown me. She showed up at my house, and I explained in person and added that God said repent, or he was going to shut the door to the ministry. God did exactly what He said, He shut the door. My friend hugged and prayed for us, and she left. A few days later, we left on our way to a new city for a new beginning.

***

My uncle and his friend loaded the truck the night before and were off before daybreak. I loaded Damien and the remainder of our things in the van, and we were on our way to the big city of Myrtle Beach. I was scared, and my family was hurt and angry. But I had to follow God's plan for my life. I had tried everything else, and nothing else seemed to work. I was torn between the known, which is my family, friends, and even the drama that I had been living and going to a place I knew nothing about and finding my own way. I mean, depending on this God everyone else knew wasn't working at least not for me. I was on a journey to find out who God was for me. I was scared as hell, but I was fed up and knew deep within me there had to be more. God was already showing himself to be strong in my life; I just needed to interpret what it all meant for me specifically. I took a deep breath, said a prayer, and hit the gas pedal, refusing to look back.

***

Damien looked at me and smiled, “What’s for breakfast?”

I said, “McDonald's.”

“Great!” he said, then he began singing, “I’m in love with the McDonald’s girl!” Both of us laughed and agreed to stop.

My uncle and his friend had stopped and were sitting down to eat breakfast to kill time.

My uncle said, “The office doesn’t open until 10 am, so we have some time on our hands. I encourage you to take your time and eat breakfast because once we get there, we have a lot to do.”

We ordered drive-through and got back on the road. The ride was pleasant. It seemed the closer we got, the greener everything seemed. My uncle was waiting for us when we got there. The manager was late opening the office, which made us later than we wanted to be because the truck had to be returned by a certain time. However, once the off-loading started, it went by fast. My living room, two bedrooms, and dining rooms were set up. The boxes were placed in the rooms where they belonged, and all I had to do was put everything up. I gave them a few dollars for lunch, thanked them, and they were headed home. It was official, we were home. Now, all I had to do was make this apartment feel like home. In about a week, everything was put up, and we settled into our routine.

However, Damien had to sleep in the bed with me for about two weeks. This allowed us to come together as husband and wife. Yes, we pulled out the box and pumped it up. I was finally able to exhale, putting everything behind us. We spent a lot of time talking about things we should have done before getting married. It made me begin to understand the man but not excuse him. However, the past was the past and I was already in the situation. I wanted to make the best of it.

We began spending a lot of time exploring our new neighborhood. We were close to everything and, therefore, could walk. There were times he would ride me on his lap. We laughed, kissed, and were falling in love once again by the grace of God. I believed the change of scenery was good for us. Since I wasn't working, both of us decided to hold up on the aid for a while. Sometimes, services can be confining because even if we wanted to go somewhere or do anything, we had to be home because of all the aides, therapists, and nurses who came. So, we started the services that were necessary and held up on the CNA. We focused on us. That didn't last long.

My daughter was the first to move down, then one of the girls I had custody of with her three children, and finally, my daughter's best friend and her two children. Ten people in a two-bedroom apartment. My daughter became Damien's aide so that she would have a job, and the other girls soon were working as well. All the children were in school or daycare. I would play school bus driver in the afternoon. Going to each class at the daycare. I would have 3 children in car seats and 2 older children who came for after-school care. This went on five days a week.

Damien loved it because those children adored him, and I now had help in the house. You see, Damien didn't have a relationship with his biological children, so these babies made his day. They would fall asleep in his arms, whether in the wheelchair or lying in bed at night. Some would always knock on the door at night to crawl in bed with us. This went on for about a year. I finally told all the girls that they needed to find their own place, and I was going to give them until tax season to make it happen. They pooled their resources and made it happen. I still helped them with the kids because they had to work. Cara eventually got another job, and she and her best friend moved in with the kids. Everything was working well; I now had family here, and they had their own place. I showed them where to go find cheap furniture, and they all had cars to get around.

I decided that it was time to bring the aide in because I was getting ready to enroll in college. I spoke with an agency, and they sent someone out for me to talk to. I explained my previous experiences and that I wouldn't tolerate any of those things anymore. I encouraged the CNA to talk to me if she had any problems, and we would work them out. Just don't get caught up running behind my husband because many have lost their jobs because of it. I explained that he was the patient, but I was the one that they needed to ask any questions.

The aide started shortly after; it wasn't long before Damien started his regular routine as before we moved.

He was hanging out all day, disrespectful, and constantly wanting to argue. As a last resort, we joined the church of my best friend's father. I was trying to do all I could. However, I was emotionally spent and, to be honest, felt like a fool. I needed to get things in order for him to be put in a facility. It was a slow process, but I knew what I had to do, and I did it. I stayed focused.

While this was going on, the girls ended up losing their apartments one by one, and I told them they needed to move back home to Columbia. They were mad, but each one made plans to do just that. I had too much going on to take on all that responsibility, especially with what was going on between me and Damien.

I thank God because he was the last one to go. I found a state-run facility that could take him.

Damien said, "I thought you were playing."

As I pulled up to the facility to drop off him along with all his stuff, I felt relieved and devastated all at the same time. Though I was leaving him, I still had his power of attorney, so as we made our way inside with his belongings, a staff member stopped me.

They said, "I will call you concerning his care."

I replied, "Thank you." Then I looked at Damien and said, "Good-bye."

I turned and walked out the door, holding back tears. I cried all the way home because the enemy had won despite how hard I tried. My entire world had fallen apart, and there was absolutely nothing I could do about it. Why did God allow this to happen? I tried everything. I prayed, fasted, and cried. I tried to be understanding of all he had gone through in his life. I even tried forgetting all the hideous things I had seen and even been told by him. Why God? Why? Isn't this what a wife is supposed to do? Why did it not work for me? I felt so angry and defeated inside. I focused on the road and turned up the music. Before long, the tears had stopped, and I was bopping my head to the oldies.

***

Looking back, I realized that I could have handled this situation better, but in truth, we oftentimes don't make the best decisions while in crisis. Anyone looking from the outside could say how they would handle a situation until it's them. It's easy to pass judgment on someone else's situation and fail to see their own flaws. For example, I stayed upset with my mom for a long time because when I told her about what happened to me concerning being molested, I wanted her to act a certain way, but she remained quiet and changed the subject. I learned some years later that she was dealing with her own trauma.

I can't tell you what she was feeling, but when I found out about Damien and his daughter, I became numb and needed to compartmentalize to get through what I needed to deal with at that time. I literally was fighting for his soul and my redemption as a Christian versus giving up and leaving, which meant I was wrong again and a failure. I needed to win for him, me, and even God. You see, I felt as though the devil had been winning all my life, and I was drawing the line in the sand, saying no, you can't take one more thing from me.

He wasn't my Boo thang; he was my husband, and I vowed to love him in good times, bad times, sickness, and health until death do us part. I think I assumed that God wanted me to be married to this man versus me wanting to be married to him. I learned there is a difference.

It wasn't that what his daughter said wasn't important, but I needed to deal with the immediate threat, not to mention that I needed to process it all. It would be a reasonable assumption after his daughter's confession that what happened between them would be enough to convict in the other situation. What if God judged us based on our past? That's why I laid it at his feet, asking that the truth be revealed. In my heart, I was mortified because I was put in a position to take the word of the man I was married to over the child who was allegedly molested. Damien confessed to what happened with his daughter, but that didn't make him guilty of what he was accused of in the other situation. I would have chosen the child because no one heard me when I went through the same thing. However, something in me knew something was off. We must be careful because we can judge an innocent person based on our pain and their past. He was guilty through admission of molesting his daughter but not about the neighbor's kid.

Reflection

We tend to view life through the eyes of our past. However, I've learned no one is all good, and no one is all bad, not you and not me. God gives grace and mercy even to those of us who others feel don't deserve it. So, ask yourself how do you view life and the people in it? Is it through the eyes of your pain or past? Or do you see through the eyes of Jesus? I personally have learned to embrace everything God says and sees concerning my life. It is only through Him that I am now victorious.

CHAPTER SIX

The 6th Hour: Moving On

Once I got home, I sat down, looked around, and began to cry uncontrollably. Once again, I was reminded that my life was in shambles. He was gone, and everywhere I looked was a reminder of what the enemy had done. I decided that I would give myself that night to have my pity party, but tomorrow would be another day. I wondered if I was supposed to be married. Lord knows I had tried to make it work, but it just didn't.

I decided that it was time to make some changes, I was alone, so it was time I embraced it. The first step was to get a smaller apartment. There was no reason to hold on to an apartment this big when all it did was remind me of what I lost. I found it in the same complex right around the corner from the old one. The thing is, I still had the same furniture but not all the space, which indicated something was wrong. Instead, everything fit neatly in my new digs. Everything that Damien couldn't take, I got rid of except for his portable ramp. I had a girlfriend who was in a wheelchair, and it would come in handy when she visited. However, when I didn't need it, I placed it in the closet, out of sight, out of mind. It didn't take long to get everything set up, and within a week, everything was in place, and I felt like I finally had my own space. One that reflected me. My sadness started to lift, and I felt inspired.

My second decision was to get rid of my van. Why should I keep a large van when it was only me? Besides, the girls had ruined the transmission, and sooner or later, it was going to put me down. So, I put it down first. I traded it in on a brand-new white Dodge Avenger. The white stood for purity. I guess in my mind, I was purifying myself and closing the door to any possibility of him coming back.

My third decision was to get back into church like I used to be. I started attending my girlfriend's church, where her father was the pastor. Damien and I had sat under him before we moved. However, he got a church here in the Myrtle Beach area not long after Damien's accident; therefore, he knew me. Before long, I was licensed and taking minister classes under him. I loved those classes, but they didn't answer certain questions for me.

One day, while talking to a friend of mine from back home, she suggested that I take online classes because not many people would be able to answer the questions I was asking.

She said, "You've acquired a hunger to know God more deeply and that you needed to experience Him in your own way.

She also cautioned me that these same classes would either make me walk away or give me a deeper revelation of who God really was. In a nutshell, they challenge what you believe.

She said, "I remember even having to defend my faith in a class I'd taken."

I didn't care. I needed to do this for me. The next morning, I googled online colleges, and Mid-American Christian University stood out the most to me. I mustered up enough nerve to call and speak with a counselor who walked me through the entire process, specifically selecting only the classes I would need to get my bachelor's degree in Christian Ministry and Counseling. Before I knew it, I was a forty-five-year-old college student. I was given a few weeks before my classes started to get familiar with the school's computer program and the honor code. Now, I had been out of school for almost thirty years and had no experience working a computer. I was lost. However, I kept at it until I was able to maneuver. I finished my prerequisites and signed up for my first class. My first subject was math. I hadn't seen this type of math in a long time, and I was already scratching my head. Now, to my benefit, I decided to take one class at a time because I had no clue as to what I was in for. This allowed me to focus on that one subject for the entire five weeks. My counselor contacted me to ensure I knew about all the support and tutorials that were available if I needed them.

She said, "Many adult students found it helpful seeing how it had been a while since they were in this type of environment. She went on to say that she would be there for me whenever I needed her."

Trust me, I needed her for technical support, tutorials, and understanding the assignments.

The first thirty days were brutal, and I cried every day it seemed. I considered quitting online classes and going into a local brick and mortar so I could reach out and touch the teacher. However, no one could accommodate my program. I would've had to go to school for eight years, attending two different colleges. I decided to stick it out, and by the third month, I was getting the hang of it, and I had started to pull my grades up. I was building a life for myself, and I was happy and working towards something that mattered to me.

It was only a short time ago that I felt I was on the edge of a nervous breakdown. I remember going to the grocery store right after Damien and I split up. I grabbed a buggy and headed into the store down my usual aisles. Before I knew it, I was reaching for items Damien normally needed. A voice within me said he's not here now. I took a deep breath and really tried to think hard about what I wanted to eat. I drew a blank. I know it sounds crazy, but I had put the needs of others before me so long that I got lost in the shuffle. I was used to eating what everyone else ate. I became so overwhelmed that I left the buggy in the middle of the aisle and left the store crying.

I've come a long way, and I was not that woman anymore. There was no Damien, no Cara, no girls, and none of their children. It was just me! I had been in that cycle of taking care of others for twenty-six years, and now it was finally my turn. God kept his promise concerning me; I walk in the favor of God and man, my income almost tripled, and I am licensed as a minister and enrolled in school to learn more about God. Things were finally looking up for me, and Lord knows I was glad about it.

Then, the day came when Damien's sister called.

She said, "You need to get to the facility as soon as you can. Something is wrong with Damien, but the nurses and doctors refused to talk to me because you are listed as his power of attorney."

I agreed and said, "I will be there as soon as I get an oil change."

She reemphasized the importance of my coming ASAP. I said, "Give me a day or two."

I got up immediately to go get my car's oil changed because it was the first time since I had bought it.

The guy at the service desk asked, "Can I help you?

I said, "Yes, I need to get my oil changed because I must go out of town unexpectedly."

He said, "Sure, but it may take a while because you don't have an appointment."

I asked, "What's a while?"

"About an hour to an hour and a half," He said.

I said, "That's fine."

He asked, "May I have your name and phone number? And are you going to stay and wait on the car or leave it?"

I said, "Wait."

He said, "Good. That will give me something good to look at."

I said, "What did you say, sir?"

He said, "Sir? I'm not that old. My name is Bobby!"

I just looked at him.

He continued, "Things can't be that bad, can they?"

I said, "No, and for once, I'm going to keep it that way."

Bobby smiled as I turned and walked away to the waiting room. In about an hour, the car was ready, and Bobby escorted me to pick up my keys.

He flirtatiously said, "This oil change is on us. See you next time."

I smiled and said, "Thank you." And I was on my way.

As I was driving home, my mind went to Bobby. He was about my height, heavy set but in a cute kind of way, not sloppy fat. He was dark-skinned with a poorly managed goatee. His clothes were wrinkled and had visible stains. His eyes were filled with crust like he had just gotten out of bed, but it was noon. However, he had a great personality and an awesome smile. I quickly shut down those thoughts and mentally prepared for the morning trip. His sister sounded frantic, and I knew something was wrong.

As Bobby's flirtatious voice reentered my thoughts, I silently whispered, "Not this time. I'm staying focused and not falling for it. Besides, I'm still married."

As I started out the next morning, I noticed a U-Haul place. An overwhelming feeling rose in me that said you're going to need it. I decided to stop and rent a cargo van just in case. I honestly didn't know what to expect, but I knew I needed to be prepared for whatever I might encounter. Besides, I didn't have a lot of time; I had a deadline to meet for school. My goal was to handle business and get back home as soon as I could so I wouldn't fall behind in my assignments. I took a deep breath, said a quick prayer, and reasoned it couldn't be that bad because I never received a phone call from the facility. While driving, my mind wondered what could possibly be going on. "Ann, stop this. There is nothing you can do about it now," I thought. So, I turned the music up, focused on the road, and before I knew it, I was pulling into the facility

As I entered the facility, I noticed a strong foul odor. However, I proceeded to the front desk to sign in. Once I signed in and received my visitor badge, I proceeded to Damien's room. He was lying in bed, playing with his phone.

I asked, "How are you doing?"

He said, "I'm doing okay."

I continued, "I received a phone call from your sister asking me to come check on you."

He responded with a kind of grunt and pointed to his hip. He pulled his blanket back, and I was able to see the green puss that had drained through his dressings. The smell was awful.

He said, "I have them all over now."

I immediately began to check him out, and he was right. They were on both hips, butt, legs, heels, and his back, all oozing green puss.

I asked, "Why didn't you call me?"

He said, "For what? You left me here."

I called the charge nurse and demanded to know what happened.

She explained, "Quadriplegics, over time, get this disease that causes their skin to easily break down. It's normal.

I cut her off and said, "There is nothing normal about this. Furthermore, no one called me about his condition. Why isn't he in a hospital?"

She tried to explain, but there was no reason for what I was looking at. No reason at all. I informed the nurse and his case worker that they had one hour to get him ready for release.

The caseworker said, "It is not possible to have him ready that soon because we are running short on staff."

I replied, "That's why his wounds look the way they do."

However, that wasn't my problem but theirs. I left to go get some loading ramps for his electric wheelchair, and I was back within the hour. A worker helped me load Damien and all his things in the van, and I was headed back home. Now Damien was still upset with me for putting him in that place, and he didn't try to hide it.

I got the silent treatment, which was fine with me. Beat the heck out of arguing. However, he broke his silence long enough to ask for McDonald's. I stopped, got him something to eat, and continued.

I explained to Damien, "I have downsized, and things are going to be different this time because I'm here not as your wife but as a friend trying to help a friend."

He agreed and said, "Our marriage was over because of what you did. It was done when you put me in the home."

I refrained from responding and focused on the road home. Praying that his healing process would be quick and that his family would take him in, seeing how his being in the facility didn't work.

We made it in about two hours and thirty minutes. I called an old friend of Damien's and mine to assist me in unloading the van and getting Damien in the house. Craig came quickly. Damien immediately perked up like nothing was wrong and began talking to Craig. We were able to get Damien out of the van and into his portable chair, where Craig pushed him into the house. Craig then came back for the electric chair, Hoyer lift, and his clothes and medical supplies. I told him to get the ramp that I used for his wife when she came over to get the electric chair in the house. He nodded. I then asked him if he could wait with Damien so I could take the van back and pick up my car. He said yes, that would give them time to catch up. By the time I returned, all of Damien's things were in the apartment, and Damien was comfortably sitting in his electric chair. I thanked Craig for helping out. He said he was happy to help anytime, waved his hand, and walked back to his apartment.

I immediately called EMS so that Damien could be seen. It didn't take any time at all for the ambulance to arrive. I gathered his medications and followed closely behind the ambulance to ensure I was able to go in with them instead of sitting in the waiting room. Damien wasn't back there no time before the doctor came in to do his assessment. He immediately admitted him. The doctor said he wouldn't have lasted much longer with the infection going untreated.

He had two different strands of infection, and one of the medications that they normally would give no longer worked, which limited his treatment options.

The doctor said, "He will be in the hospital for quite a while to first get the infections under control and to work on all the wounds he has. I put an order in for a special bed that will help with the healing of his wounds. I also ordered the dressings to be changed three times a day until the green puss stops."

The doctor also ordered a high protein, low carb diet, which would help his wounds heal faster. His medications had to be adjusted as well because his blood sugars were through the roof. I realized he was in good hands, so I decided to leave to get some things done.

The doctor said, "You will need to get his services set up so that when he gets out of the hospital, they can start immediately."

Because of the severity of his wounds, he could not be released until he had everything he needed at the house. The doctor started the process by writing the orders for his bed, home health, and wound care nurses. I also contacted the case worker for the Department of Disability and Special Needs, who started the ball rolling on her end for medical supplies. I also requested a different type of Hoyer Lift, which would make it easy for me and the aide to transfer him.

At the end of the second week, the doctor said, "It's time that we discuss his care once he gets home. Damien will be going home with an I.V. antibiotic that you will need to administer twice a day and for his wound care twice a day, four days a week."

I took a deep breath and said, "Okay. Is someone going to train me to do all of this?"

The doctor said, "Yes, the wound care nurse will also help."

I nodded.

Damien looked at me, and I said, "Everything is going to be just fine."

I trained with the nurses at the hospital for about three days on giving him his antibiotics through IV and caring for his wounds. They said I did well and would be fine taking care of him at home. They reported to the doctor, and he was finally discharged.

Everything that he needed was in place and started the afternoon he returned home. The wound care nurse watched me as I did his wounds first. She smiled. Then I hooked up his IV and set it so that he would get just the right dosage in an hour's time. When it finished, I went slowly through the steps so that she could observe. She couldn't believe it.

She said, "You missed your calling."

I said, "His life depends on me doing it right, so I paid attention."

She said, "He's lucky to have you."

I replied, "Thank you for being patient with me."

She smiled and said, "You're helping us."

She left for the night. I checked with Damien to see if he needed anything, and I went to bed. As I fell asleep, I took a deep breath and thanked God for the aide who was coming the next morning.

Monique was supposed to be there at 9 am, but it was now 9:30. She was late on the first day. I'm just glad that Damien was still sleeping. Monique showed up five minutes later. She stared at me, and I stared at her. It was almost like we instantaneously hated each other. However, I needed an aide, and she needed the job, so we sat down to talk. I explained to her all the problems I had with other aides and that I was not going to tolerate them anymore. I needed someone dependable. However, I know that things come up, but I needed her to talk to me, not Damien. I would work with her in any way I could. The second thing I needed was to know what time she was going to report to work. I told her that Damien normally got up between 9:30 and 10:30 am. If she was there by the time he got up, I was okay. She said that 10 would work for her, and I agreed. I went on to tell her that she would need to cook for him sometimes, but normally, it would already be done. She nodded. I told her she would be responsible for keeping his room clean, vacuuming as needed, and for his personal care, such as bathing and assisting with hygiene. Finally, she would be responsible for giving his meds, although they would already be separated. She nodded in agreement. She then took a few minutes to tell me about herself, and I began to walk her through his routine. I told her that once she got the hang of it, I would probably make myself scarce because, though she was there, he would call me all day, and I would never get anything done.

Things went well that day, so I asked if five hours during the day and then two at night would work for her. She said, "To be honest, that won't work for me because I don't live close to you. I would rather do all my hours at one time, but I will make it work if I need to." I appreciated her honesty and told her so because it would have only caused a problem later. I told her I'd pray about it, and we'd talk in the mornings.

I prayed and decided to let her do all the hours at once. That would give me more time to accomplish what I needed to during the day, such as classes, and then if he had a doctor's appointment, she wouldn't be pushed to get back in time. This would even give me more freedom at night if I wanted to go to a church service or something. I wouldn't need to leave and come home for the aide to put him to bed. It was a fair swap! So, I agreed and told her the next morning.

This was a game-changer. Monique caught on fast, and I was out and about before I knew it. My grades began to soar, and before I knew it, I had earned my associate's degree. I was well on my way to my bachelor's, and nothing was going to stand in my way. I had tasted victory and liked the way it felt. I was motivated.

Taking care of Damien at night was becoming more and more challenging. It was almost like he was looking for a reason to fight. I guess he realized that I was moving on with my life. He complained that he was stuck at the house all the time while I was out doing God knows what. I said, "I'm either at the library working on my school assignments or volunteering at the church. I'm not running the streets."

He said, "Yeah, right!"

His behaviors spilled over into the morning while Monique was trying to care for him. He would scream that she was hurting him. No matter what she did, he was just awful. I remember one day, he wanted to go out onto the main road to go to Walmart, which was 3 miles away across a busy highway. She wouldn't let him out. She called me and said that he was really carrying on and was threatening to call the police on her for kidnapping him. I packed my computer and told her I was on the way.

By the time I had gotten there, the police were there, and he did tell them that both of us were kidnapping him.

The police asked, "Who are you?"

I responded, "I am his wife, and she is his aide."

The officer said, "He has a sound mind, and if he wants to go, let him."

We said, "Yes, sir!"

I said to the officer, "I need you to hear what I am about to say to him."

He said, "Yes, ma'am."

I said, "I have done everything that I can to take care of you. At every turn, you fight me, so if you go, know I'm not coming looking for you."

He nodded.

The police asked, "Do you understand what she is saying?

He said, "Yes sir!" and rolled away.

I asked Monique to stay until her shift was over, just in case he returned.

She said, "That's fine, but I must report it to my supervisor."

I said, "Most definitely!"

Both of us were still in shock from the events that unfolded that day. However, we brushed it off and went about our day. She cleaned his room, and I worked on my assignments.

Damien returned later that day after Monique had left. I acted as if nothing happened because, honestly, I was tired and simply didn't care to get into it with him.

He said, "I'm hungry."

So, I fixed his food and gave him something to drink.

I asked, "Is there anything else you need before I go to finish my schoolwork?"

He looked strangely and said, "No."

I said, "Just call me when you're done eating, and I will come get your plate."

He nodded and started to eat. About thirty minutes later, he called and said," I'm done. I want to go to bed." I nodded and quietly undressed him, transferring him to the bed.

I asked, "Are you ready for your nightly meds?"

He said, "No, it's too soon."

"Just let me know when you're ready," I said.

"Can I get the remote, he asked?"

"Sure, I responded!"

I handed him the remote as I went to finish my assignment. About an hour later, he called and wanted his medication, which I gave to him. Then, I covered him up and said good night. He stared at me, I guess wondering what was really going on because I wasn't saying anything. I got myself ready for bed and fell fast asleep.

The next morning, Monique came, and I told her I had an appointment and I would be back as soon as I could. I went on to say, "Damien is still sleeping,"

She mentioned that after the day they had had before, she was just going to let him sleep, and I understood that.

As I walked out the door, I heard the Lord say, "Go by McDonald's and pick up two breakfast sandwiches.

I didn't understand right then and there, but I obeyed.

Once I got the sandwiches, the Lord said, "Give one of the sandwiches to the guy at the front desk."

I said, "What guy?"

The Lord said, "You will know him when the time comes."

I agreed. The same guy that flirted with me before was sitting at the counter.

God said, "him!"

I walked up to the counter and told him why I was there. Once he got me signed in, I said, "On the way here, the Lord instructed me to get a second sandwich for you."

He said, "Really?"

I said, "Yes, here it is."

He said, "That was nice of you."

I said, smiling, "I'm just being obedient to God."

He said, "Thank you, this really made my day."

I said, "You're welcome, but know God has you on His mind today."

I could feel him looking at me as I walked to the waiting room.

In about an hour, he appeared in the doorway and said, "I bet you don't remember my name?"

I said, No, I don't!

He said, "Bobby."

I said, "Is my car ready, Bobby, or are you around here just to see what I'm doing?"

He said, "Both!"

He escorted me to the counter to pay. Every time he would hand me my keys, he would pull them away from me playfully.

I said, 'Can you please give me my keys."

He said, "You are always so serious."

I said, "Yeah, you're right. Life is hard right now."

He said, "Well, I just wanted to thank you again for what you did."

I said, "It was only a sandwich."

He said trust me, it was more than that."

I said, "Really?

He said, "You aren't the only one having a rough time right now, and what you did really brighten my day."

I said, "I'm glad, and I pray things get better." We both smiled, and I left.

About fifteen minutes later, I noticed a weird number calling; it was Bobby.

I said, "And how did you get my number? "

He reminded me, "You gave it to make the appointment."

I said, "Oh yeah, I remember. Is something wrong with my car?"

"No, he said I just really want a friend."

I said, "Look, I'm married and not looking for any drama."

He said, "I am too, but we are separated at the time." In fact, I had just filed for divorce three months ago.

"I'm so sorry!" I said. "I understand because I'm headed in the same direction."

He said, "I understand now. That's why you looked and acted the way you did every time you came in. "

In my mind, I said, this was the beginning of a friendship that I was desperate for. I started to pick his brain about things my husband said and did, and he told me the truth about men and women from his perspective.

Bobby became my best friend rather quickly. We were always on the phone laughing. He was a breath of fresh air. I felt safe because both of us understood the situation, and neither tried to go any further. One day, Damien heard me laughing and wanted to know who I was talking to. I told him because there was nothing to it.

He immediately got an attitude, saying, "You're always on the phone with him."

I said, "He is just a friend; no more. Honestly, if it was something more, I wouldn't be talking in front of you." This seemed to heighten Damien's insanity.

Monique was on the verge of quitting because of the arguing and stress that was in the house. It didn't matter what was said or done; he made life miserable.

"Monique, I understand, but please try to hang on at least until I get some things together," I said.

She responded, "I'll try!"

On that day I began to make phone calls to his family and then facilities, my marriage was over, and I was done going through this foolishness.

I instructed him of my plans, and he said, "I'm not moving."

Listen, "You're not on my lease, and your wounds are healing, so I am just going to get things in order so that I can go on with my life."

He went silent. I decided to wait to write the eviction notice so I could run it concurrent with him going into an institution if his family didn't step up.

Monique lasted a few more weeks but eventually asked to be reassigned, and there was no one to take her place because the agency knew that he wouldn't be there too much longer. Damien tried to make my life a living hell. He was so mean even though I was now the one bathing him, cleaning his poop, dressing him, and cooking, just to name a few things.

I remember him yelling, "No one wants you but me. So, I can treat you any way I want. What are you going to do but fuss and take it? "

I couldn't even believe what I was hearing.

What he didn't know was that I had contacted a facility that was willing to take him in sixty days. I handed him his eviction notice and informed him he was leaving in sixty days, whether he had a place or not.

He said, "You can't put me out because of my disability."

I said, "I know, that's why I found some place for you to go."

He became irate, saying, "You can't make me go anywhere."

"I'm done arguing with you. You are not on my lease, and you have to go, period."

He asked to be let outside, and I did. He stayed gone for a while but returned calm.

After letting him in, I gave him his food and later got him ready for bed just as if nothing happened.

I told him, "The family is having a cookout this weekend, and I want to go."

He said, "That sounds great!"

" I will start getting our things together tomorrow after I get you up."

He said, "I'm not going to get up tomorrow. I'm staying in."

I said, "We'll see in the morning.

He said, "Good night. "

I said the same, cut the light out, and went to bed.

Damien slept late the next day, which allowed me to take advantage of the peace and quiet. I finished my school assignments and started on his lunch. I heard him call my name, and I went to see what he wanted.

I said, "You must've been tired!

"Yes," he said. He then asked for something to eat, and he took his pills.

"Are you getting up?"

"No, I'm just going to watch TV in bed today."

I said, "Well, I'm going to clean the kitchen and then start packing. Let me know if you need anything."

"Ok, that's fine," he said, nodding his head.

The day went smoothly and peacefully; not one thing went wrong.

The next morning, Damien woke up early.

I asked, "Are you ready for me to get you ready so that we could head home?"

He said, "Yes!"

As soon as I got him in his chair, he started to complain that he wasn't feeling well.

"What's wrong?" I asked.

"My stomach hurts," he said.

"But you were fine a few minutes ago," I replied.

"Go and leave me here alone," he pleaded.

"That's not going to happen. You know I have business to take care of on Monday, and the family cookout is all weekend, not to mention I've already packed the suitcase. All I had to do is load everything up and then put you in the car."

Damien insisted he wasn't going and wanted me to call EMS.

I said, "No, because you're fine!"

Before I knew it, he was on the phone, and EMS was on their way. In about ten minutes, they were at the door. I let them in, and he explained what was going on with him.

I told them, "He is faking it because he wants to stay home in the apartment all weekend by himself, and I wasn't allowing it."

They said, "We have to take him in because he could be hurt."

I said, "OK, but I won't be here when he returns. I have a hotel room waiting in Columbia for us; his bags are packed, and I was getting ready to load everything and him in the car." I went on to explain that he knew I had business to take care of there, and he agreed to go.

They said, "We understand."

I gave them my phone number, and they left with him. I unpacked his things and left soon after.

I went on with the festivities of the day, not knowing what was going on with Damien. After everything was over, I checked my phone, and it was the police department calling. I called them immediately to see what was going on.

They called, saying, "You have abandoned a vulnerable adult and need to return as soon as possible."

I explained that I would not be back until Monday because I had important business with my daughter that Damien knew about but changed his mind at the last minute. I told them I explained it to Damien, I explained it to EMS, and now I was explaining it to them, the police. "I will deal with it all when I return," I said.

The police agreed, and I hung up. Shortly after, Damien called and was crying, begging me to return because they were talking about locking me up.

I said, "I'm not coming back until I finish what I came to do."

He said, "I tried to tell the truth, but they don't believe me. They think you left me here intentionally. I told them I lied so I could stay in the apartment all weekend by myself."

He said, "I tried to get the maintenance guys to let me in, but I wasn't on your lease, so they had to take me back to the hospital, which prompted the police to be called."

I said, "Okay, I will deal with it when I get home."

"Please, hurry, I didn't mean for it to go this far.

I went straight to the hospital that Monday, and the police was waiting there for me. I once again explained to them what happened, and I was given a summons to appear in court. Damien was released, and we went home. I didn't say a word; I just went about my regular routine as if nothing had happened. Damien was confused because he was looking for me to act like a fool. The truth is it was just another confirmation that the decision I had made was correct. Separate!

A few days later, I went to court, and the judge's mind was already made up. They were ready to take me into custody when Damien's case worker spoke up and said, "Judge, I know this is going to sound strange, but Ann didn't do anything. Damien confessed to lying about being sick so he could stay in the apartment all weekend by himself. We also spoke to the ambulance driver, who confirmed that she said she had business in Columbia. They also said they saw the suitcase packed with her things as well as his, and all she had to do was close it and load it. We also talked to the maintenance guys at the complex. They knew them both and verified what happened on the day in question when Damien tried to get in." The caseworker said in this case, there was no abuse. "Damien orchestrated all of this and was upset because he wanted to be alone in the apartment for the weekend. He didn't realize all of this would happen, which caused Ann all these problems."

The judge was in disbelief.

The caseworker said, "I know, it was shocking to us as well, but it is true. We verified it all!" As the judge was getting ready to make her rule, the police asked to be heard. She allowed it. He requested that the case be left open for a while because he believed that there was more to the story than what was being told. The judge agreed and asked his caseworker to follow up with home visits. As I started out of the courtroom, his caseworker said, "I will be calling to make an appointment to come by."

I said, "No, don't call. Just come; that way, you can see firsthand what's going on."

Within a couple of days, the caseworker was knocking on the door. I opened the door and invited him in.

He said, "I am here to look around and talk to Damien."

I said, "You can look around, but Damien is not here."

He said, "What do you mean he is not here?

I said, "Exactly the way it sounds. He left!"

He said, "Where is he?"

I said, "Probably in Kroger or someplace he can get on Wi-Fi. "

He said, "Well, I'm going to look for him."

I spoke. "I will be here."

In about an hour and a half, he came back and said that he was up at Kroger. His caseworker was shocked that he would go into traffic, placing himself in danger just to be out and about. I smiled and said, "Believe it."

He asked, "Are you concerned?"

"Not anymore," I said.

He shook his head, saying, "When Damien disappears, we need you to call the police for your protection. I already see some questionable behavior from him. I can't understand why a man would rather be in the street than home where it's clean, he has food, and someone loves him." His environment and situation are quite different than what we first thought. I nodded and escorted him to the door. He wished me a good day and left.

Now Bobby and I were becoming closer, especially with everything going on with Damien. He became my rock because, honestly, I was ready to bust Damien upside his head. All I knew was I was counting down the time for him to leave. I just needed to keep it together until then. I remember a day Bobby was on the phone, and Damien was going off on me.

Bobby said, "Let me talk to him, but first put me on speaker."

I did as he asked!

He said, "Damien, I have fallen in love with Ann, and you need to thank God that she cares enough about you to allow you to stay there until a place can be found for you. You no longer have to worry about loving or caring for her because that is now my job, and as soon as you and Ann are divorced, we will be married. But in the meantime, I will be the reason she smiles!"

Damien was shocked and rolled away. By 8:00 pm, he still hadn't come home, so I called the police to report him missing. The police came, took a report, and asked to see a picture of him. I also gave them a description of his chair.

They asked, "Did we have a fight, or was there anything that happened to make him want to leave?

I said, "No. He normally would stay gone all day, but never this late. However, his caseworker has gone looking for him and found him at Kroger. I said he is anywhere there is Wi-fi."

I waited until 9:00 p.m. and went to bed.

The next day, his case worker showed up and asked to speak to him. I said, "He's not here, and to be honest, he didn't come home last night. I followed your instructions and contacted the police."

The caseworker said he would go looking for him but would make sure he would document his behavior for the court.

Damien showed up three days later. I contacted the police department, who had to come to verify that I hadn't abused him to close their missing person's report out. I left them alone so they could speak freely with him. Within a couple of hours, his caseworker showed up to find out what was going on. His response was always the same, "because that's what he wanted to do." This behavior went on for months.

I remember the last time the police came, they asked, "Damien, why are you putting this woman through all of this?"

He said, "Because I can. No one else is going to put up with it."

He couldn't see me, but I heard what he said, and what love I had for him in that moment was gone.

I decided to take a cruise because I was tired and just needed a break, not to mention I needed time away from the drama. I needed to have an emotional funeral. I was done in my head, and now I needed my heart to follow suit. I talked to Damien's caseworker, who provided care for him until I returned. I called a friend, and before I knew it, we were off. She needed a vacation, and I just needed to breathe.

I was also falling in love with Bobby, and I was afraid. I was praying that by the time I got back, the feelings would be gone. I wanted to deal with one thing before getting involved in another. However, Bobby had become my savior. He swooped in, and my life changed for the better. I had never met anyone that attentive. He listened and expected nothing in return. I was fighting it every step of the way. He was a dream come true during a nightmare. Truthfully, I was freaking out, and maybe time on the ocean would give me perspective.

The more I was away from Bobby, the more I missed him. I finally broke down and called him from the ship, and he was so happy to hear from me. We talked every day! I finally revealed to him how I was feeling and that I had been trying to hide it and even fight it because of my situation.

He said I already knew how you were feeling, and I'm glad because I feel the same way.

We decided to meet the day after I returned to talk about it. I decided that day, but I just didn't realize it at the time.

The trip was relaxing, and what I needed to get me through the rest of the time with Damien. He was within weeks of leaving, and I just needed to remain focused if I didn't want to go to jail. This negro was pulling out all stops to piss me off. One day, he had a young lady on speaker phone; she heard me ask him if he needed anything?

He said, "No!

And as I went to walk away, I heard the girl on the phone say, "Who is that bitch keep coming in the room?"

He said, "Don't pay that bitch any attention."

I saw the jail cell closing on me. I started hitting and tearing up everything in the room. I wanted to tear his head off. Instead, I had a better idea. I walked out of his room and made a phone call.

Bobby came over, and we finally talked about where we wanted things to go. We had been friends for about a year, not acting on how each of us felt. But that night, I was not waiting for him to make the first move. Before I knew it, I had jumped on him, and all the stress I had been feeling for the last five years was released. I couldn't believe that it had been five years since a man was able to make love to me the way he did. I think it was even better because Damien was in his room. I remember Bobby putting his hands over my mouth. I wasn't trying to be loud, but the truth is I was done, and I didn't care whether Damien heard it or not. We were living two different lives, and I was tired of being lonely and miserable. Bobby was shocked, and to be honest, I was too! I was shocked, but I wasn't sorry it happened. For the first time in a long time, somebody was taking care of me in the way I needed and at the time I needed. After Bobby left, I went and checked on Damien, who had put his headphones on so he could listen to music.

I asked, "Do you need anything?"

"No," he said.

I said, “I’m headed to bed.

"Good night.”

I went and sat on the side of the bed, thinking about what I had just done. I waited for conviction to set in, and it didn’t come at that moment. So, I went and got in the shower, got dressed for bed, and as soon as my head hit the pillow, I was out.

A week later, Damien’s caseworker called, “We are closing the abuse case out.”

I said, “Good, just in time for him to be moving. You see, he only has another week here with me.”

I decided to ask Damien what his plans were?

He said, “I’m not going into a home.”

I said, “I’m not going to argue with you. I’m fine if you have someplace to go, but I’m just done. “

All day that day, he was on the phone trying to get his family to take him in. He was growing more and more angry every day. He called the police to see if I could put him out.

They said, “You are not on her lease; therefore, if she gives you proper time to move, you have to go. However, you cannot leave him on the street,”

I said, “No, I found a facility that is willing to accept him.”

He then looked at Damien and said, “Then you would have to go to the facility or find a place of your own and be able to take you and all your property by the date she gave you.”

I said, “I gave him sixty days to find a place.”

He said, "Then she can legally put you out despite your disability."

He was not happy. You could see the hopelessness settle in, and he got quiet.

I decided the next day to go and speak with an attorney. I was told that if I left him and filed for divorce, he would get the judge's pity, and I could end up paying over $500 a month.

I said, "Really, despite everything that has happened." He said, "Yes, because you're able-bodied and can go make money and build a life for yourself. He can't!"

I said, "Thank you," and I left. On the way home, I said, "God, I trust you, and he's got to go!"

Moving day came, and he didn't fight me on it. Yes, he was angry, but he knew that I was going to do what was best for me. I rented a van and loaded all of his things. I made sure there was nothing left because he wasn't coming back. When they got him settled, I told him that I would always be his friend as long as he didn't fight me on the divorce. I said being married didn't work, but maybe our friendship could be saved. He agreed, and we have been friends ever since. We were divorced one year later.

***

Years later, he told me that he didn't think I was serious about leaving him there. He thought that I was just trying to punish him. I said no, it was time for both of us to live our lives and know that if you ever need me, I will be there, but we can never live together again. We've been divorced now for almost six years. The last time I talked to him, he was out of the facility and living with his boo-thang. I'm so happy for him.

Damien and I have become good friends. We talk every now and again, and I go to check on him every now and again when I'm in Columbia. However, our relationship has changed dramatically. I no longer take responsibility for him. It took me a long time to get to this point because I felt guilty. I was able to walk away from the marriage where he couldn't physically. However, I kept my promise to always be his friend, and he does the same by checking on me from time to time.

Reflection

Looking back, I made my assignment my husband. I encourage you today to know your role in the lives of the people around you. I knew what it was like to feel like a failure, so I wanted to be there for Damien because no one was there for me. So, I ask you today to take inventory of the people in your life. Ask yourself the following questions:

1. Why are they there? Is it God or you trying to change them, fix them, or support them? It matters!
2. What is your role concerning them?
3. Do they reciprocate or are they always taking?

Once you evaluate your relationships, you may need to make some adjustments based on your answers. As I said previously, this can be a difficult process, but you must be willing to put your own healing and deliverance above others. The same God that is healing and delivering you will do the same for them. I needed to stop being baby Jesus, and now I have.

CHAPTER SEVEN

The 7th Hour: Thou Art with Me

Before Damien left, I started to get more involved in church leadership and to be honest, it wasn't what I thought it was. However, Damien decided he wanted us to attend another church because he felt he wasn't being fed where we were going. I called my pastor and informed him of our intention to leave the church. He seemed stunned. I think he took the reason Damien wanted to leave personally. However, he reluctantly agreed.

Later that day, his daughter, my best friend, called and said that her dad wanted to meet with me. He wanted me to return the license. I agreed to the day because, honestly, I had so much going on until it simply didn't matter anymore. I prayed that this move would be what

Damien needed to get himself back in line with God, which would make my life better. The day I returned, the meeting felt more like an ambush. I was attacked. I listened but stood firm on my decision. I remember the pastor's last words as I walked out the door.

"How are you going to listen to your husband when you are the one called?"

I looked back and said, "I thought my husband was my first ministry?" I followed up with the fact that his wife has always stood beside him in his decisions, so when Damien said he wanted to go someplace where he could learn about God, I had to do whatever was necessary as his wife.

He brought into question the shape of my marriage.

I agreed and said, "But that doesn't stop him from being the head. God created the order, and I wasn't walking away from God, just the church. I told him it wasn't about me but the soul of my husband, and if he felt he wasn't learning anything there, I was going to take him where he could."

I wished them well and walked out the door!

Though I was at this new ministry, I had been wounded by the pastor because I had been around them most of my adult life at this point, and I could not believe what I had just experienced with him. His daughter was my best friend, and they acted like I was an employee who had just quit my job. They were angry, like I did something to them personally.

Though Damien and I started the services together, he was gone now, and I was stuck with an emptiness he once held. I quickly got involved in singing in the choir and working in the food pantry.

The Apostle approached me one day, saying that he had received a call from my previous pastor, and he only had great things to say.

I said, "Really? The last conversation I had with him did not go well. In fact, he was very disrespectful to me for leaving and joining this ministry."

The Apostle said, "He had been watching me and wanted to license and ordain me."

I said, "No!"

He said, "I'm going to give you some time, but God's will must be done. You can't stay in one place because of what happened."

He gave me another two months, and right before church got out one Sunday, he called me up front and did it. No bells, no whistles!

I remember him saying, "I know that you are still processing a lot of what happened to you, but God called you, and He will heal and deliver you. He will also use you greatly because he knows your heart and desire to serve Him. You are more concerned about serving God than you are about serving man. He said you did right by your husband and God, don't worry about man."

I smiled and, on that day, put it behind me.

It wasn't long before I was the pastor's right hand. He made me Director of Operations. Anything dealing with the running of the ministry had to come through me. I had the church credit card and was asked to sit on the finance committee. I declined and said, "It is unethical to spend money and balance the books." I volunteered full-time in the ministry. My life was starting to look up. I felt complete. I was working for the Lord, and the past was becoming a distant memory.

Bobby started to complain that he felt I was spending too much time around the church and the pastor. I explained that I was only doing what I felt God was calling me to do.

"Yeah, but I need to see you, and you're never home," he said.

"So, when do you want to come, Bobby?"

He said, "Tonight after I get off work."

I agreed and proceeded with my day.

Bobby never showed up, and he never called. I was confused because this was his idea. We hadn't seen each other in quite a while, and I thought he was excited; at least, he sounded excited. Something in my Spirit didn't sit well, so I tried to call, and his phone went straight to voicemail. I left a message wanting to know what happened. I was tired from my day and decided to go to bed and get some rest. I was mad, but there was nothing I could do about it in that moment. So, I turned over and went to sleep.

The morning came quickly, and I was off and running before I knew it. I heard my phone ringing, and I knew it was him. I took a deep breath and answered. He immediately began to explain. In my heart, I saw the red flag, but I didn't want to let go of the dream I was experiencing, and he was there in the middle of the nightmare. He apologized and said he had an emergency concerning one of his sons. He vowed that he would come tonight if I would let him. I agreed. Bobby made me feel so safe and loved until yes was my only answer. I loved him and wanted the relationship to work.

We didn't see each other that much but talked on a regular basis. He worked 10-hour days, and I volunteered from sunup to sundown myself. This went on for about another year and a half when I decided it was time for Bobby and I to have a serious talk about what was going to happen between us.

Bobby said, "I love you and that there is no one else for me. I just need a little more time because my wife is causing issues for me in trying to get the divorce."

I told him, "I will not continue seeing you if you're not going to get a divorce." I explained that I knew what it was like to be a wife and to be disrespected by other women who disrespect you just to be with your husband. I said, "I will not do that to another woman. It was painful to me, and I won't inflict that kind of pain on anyone. Besides, she is your wife, not me!"

Bobby went on to say, "It is not about my wife but the kids. You see, my dad's lack of support for me and my siblings was hard on my mom. So, being the oldest meant I had to get a job at an early age to keep a roof over our heads and food for us to eat."

I told him, "I understand, but I am already sinning to be with you. You said you were getting a divorce, and that's why I fought not to fall in love with you. I just knew something like this was going to happen. I just knew it!"

He said, "Calm down. You are the one I want, and I want to prove it to you."

"How?"

He said, "What about a baby?"

I said, "No, I don't want to talk about that because of the miscarriages I've had. I told him that I had accepted that that was not going to happen for me and that I didn't want to try just to be heartbroken again.

He said, "I think you still want to have a baby, but put it out of your mind because of the miscarriages. He wiped the tears from my eyes and began to kiss me."

I said, "So, what are you saying you want to go half on a baby?"

He said, "Yes, and that was the first night we tried. While making love, he whispered that he wanted to heal me from all the things that broke me, and this was a good place to start. He said you will be my wife, and we will raise our child together."

Every reservation I had was gone, and I stopped fighting and fell completely in love with him. One day, while at the church, Bobby called because I had been there working in the food pantry all day, and I was now waiting for Bible study to start. The Apostle walked outside where I was and began yelling at me to get off the phone and come inside. I said, "I'm coming. Is it time for the study to start?"

He said, "No, but you need to be inside, not outside on the phone."

This was strange because he had never acted that way before. Bobby went off, saying, "This man does not act like your pastor but your man. I don't like it, and I'm about to come up to the church and show him who your man is."

I said, "Look, I'm sure he didn't mean it that way."

Bobby demanded I talk to him before he did.

After the study, I pulled the apostle to the side and asked him not to do that again because it caused issues between me and my man. He looked at me without ever responding.

I said, "Look, your conduct was inappropriate, and if someone had heard you, they would have gotten the wrong impression."

He smiled and said, "It's my job to protect you, and that's what I'm doing."

I shook my head and left.

As I got ready for bed, I started to replay the events of the day. I had to admit to myself that it was kind of weird, but I knew nothing was going on, so I dismissed it and went straight to sleep. Bobby and I talked all the time, but we really didn't see each other much; however, I told him that I thought I was pregnant. He didn't believe me because it had only been once since we tried. I told him that I felt like something was wrong and was on the way to his job.

He came out after about fifteen minutes, and as he walked over to the car, he said, "Oh my God, my wife is going to kill me."

I said, "What did you say?"

He said, "My wife and children are going to kill me."

I said, "But you said you were separated and were just waiting to sign the papers."

The tears began to run down my face, and I realized I had been a fool. My emotions were raw, but I cranked the car and drove off without speaking a word.

As I drove Bobby was blowing my phone up. He left messages on my voicemail saying he just needed me to wait until his last child got out of school. I didn't respond. I got home and cried because I was almost three months pregnant and alone. I literally had a conversation with myself, trying to understand how I could let this happen. Why would he bring a child into this madness, and why didn't I see it?

Bobby tried to reach out to me, but I refused to talk to him. I lost the baby due to stress, and I hated him for it. Another miscarriage. A part of me was mad as hell, and then the other side was glad because I was no longer a young girl capable of taking care of a child on my own. I did that when I was in my twenties and no more. I hated Bobby, but I hated myself more. That man strung me along for six years on broken promises. I don't even know how I let that happen. I guess he decided to just give me space. His calls got few in between. He even stopped leaving messages. I was miserable, and I didn't trust anyone after that. It was another two years before I talked to him again. He wanted to know what happened. I told him it was in the past and really didn't matter. "All I know is that my life has moved on, and I'm not looking back," I said.

He said, "What about the baby?"

I said, "You will be glad to know that I lost it!"

He started to get emotional, and I hung up. He called back to ask why I hung up.

I said I'm not interested in fake tears.

He said, "Wait. YOU LEFT ME!"

I said, "Really, Bobby, so I was supposed to be the side chick, and you see your child when you feel like it. That's not what we talked about."

He once again brought up what he went through with his father.

I said, "I understand, but now you can be there for your wife and children. Make the most of it because it came at a high price. At least you can go home and play with your babies. Mine is dead. So please do not call me again."

Bobby was mad, but I was furious at myself. I couldn't believe I allowed myself to get caught up in this mess. The problem was I was learning to hear from God but instead believed a lie from the devil. I had two prophets describe him and say that he was indeed my husband. I felt like it was a done deal because God's prophet spoke it. Boy, was I wrong, and this time, it almost cost me my mind. Things came on subtle until I had no defense against them. Even as I type, I know that being in that situation was wrong, but it felt right. I was what you call a real fool for this man because I would hear God tell me to do certain things for him, and I would help him buy school clothes for his children. The funny part is I never felt sorry about that. I just believed him to the point of getting pregnant. I realized something in the end. I looked at him as my savior because he gave me strength to get out of a bad situation in return for me being in a worse situation with him. I was done with this creation called man!

While all of that was going on, the apostle's wife got sick with cancer, and I started to go out to see her. I would lay on her bed and do my homework. She just wanted me close to her. Sarah was such a sweet lady, and I had grown very close to her. I remember one day she asked, "Will God heal me?"

I said, "Yes, but I didn't tell her that it would not be on this side."

She was the first assignment God gave me to help someone transition to Him. Sarah was afraid that she would not make it to heaven because of things that went on in her marriage. However, she confided in me, and I led her through a prayer of repentance. She looked at me and said, "I'm ready." As her son walked in, she visited with him and her husband, and she left to be with the Lord two days later. When reality set in, I could not believe the hurt I felt. She was the coolest white woman I ever knew. Sarah taught me that love was color blind.

It wasn't long after Sarah's funeral that the apostle announced his engagement to his assistant. The church was still grieving over Sarah, and the apostle needed me to smooth things over with everyone. I told him that they were grown, and if it was what God said, then so be it. A church meeting was called, and the proposal was made public. It was such a hostile environment. The tension in the room was unbearable. I congratulated them and went home. I could feel that something was not right but could not put my finger on it. So, I went home that night and prayed, asking God to reveal what I needed to see.

I got up the next morning and sat on the side of the bed. I heard the Lord say, "Go to your bank and ask them about using the church's credit card, which is in the name of the deceased spouse." I got up immediately and went and talked to one of the branch managers at my bank that I knew. I was informed that I could be prosecuted for using Sarah's card, and she was deceased. She said, "He gave you the card, but you are the one signing for the church purchases, so you would be liable, not him. She went on to say that he could open an account in his name or my name as a user of the card."

I was outraged!

I thanked her for the information and went straight to him. I returned the credit card and resigned from the church that day. I saw him later, and he said that he told everyone that I left because I was jealous of him getting married to his assistant.

I said, "They all know better than that. Sarah was my friend, and I loved her, and I would never disrespect her. However, I wish you two the best because Sarah is gone, and you, too, deserve to be happy." I asked him if he wanted his license and ordination certificate back, but he said, "No, God called you, so it's yours."

I thanked him and went about my way.

I stayed home for about six months to allow the Lord to deal with me. I was hurt and broken over the miscarriage, the breakup, the position the apostle put me in, and Sarah's death. I just needed a minute to get it together. However, while at home, I formed an outreach called "I am my sister's keeper." I found that there are a lot of women going through things such as sexual abuse of any kind, drug addictions, depression, low self-esteem, cooking classes, and relationship issues. If you can name it, we dealt with it on some level. We also got together once a year and cooked at the community kitchen. We also made homeless indigent bags. I needed to find something empowering to do, or I was going to lose my mind. There were no bells or whistles, just women sitting down, talking, and crying most of the time. We did whatever was necessary to get our breakthrough. We taught each other through life experience, and then I tied their situations to the solutions God gave through the Word of God. It was and still is quite effective, thank God.

Once the six months were up, God instructed me to go to a specific missionary Baptist church. I knew someone who attended, so I went with the intention of being healed by God. I didn't care about leadership. I just needed God to do the work in me. However, a friend of mine who was a minister had already spoken to the pastor about the work I was doing at my last church. When I stood to introduce myself as a visitor, he said yes, I heard about you. I smiled and nodded, and sat down. The Lord spoke to me and said, "Give a certain woman a Word from me." I obeyed, and she started to cry. She said, "Only God could have told you those things. You gave me the answers to my prayers." I said, "Amen."

The next Sunday, the pastor dismissed service, and a lady came up to be prayed for. The Lord said, "Cast the demon out of her." I obeyed and began to do as God instructed. All the church leadership was standing around looking to see what I was going to do. When the demon came out of the woman, she looked ten years younger. They all stood in amazement, and the woman thanked me.

I said, "Thank God, it's His Spirit that worked through me."

She said, "I had been dealing with that for a while, and I now look different and feel different."

I said, "Give God all the glory!"

The lady began to praise God for delivering her. The pastor and first lady said, "We need you here, and you don't have to join the church."

I nodded in agreement and began coming on the regular. I joined the church within a month and immediately got on the choir. Within three months, I was added to the praise team by the pastor. After about a year, the pastor asked me about joining the leadership team as a minister.

I said, "I really am not here for that. I just want to be here."

He said, "Listen, the past didn't kill you, so it's time to move forward in the things of God. Get over it. I understand; I'm not minimizing what you went through, but I am saying you made it. Don't allow the past to hold you hostage."

I agreed and started attending ministers' meetings.

***

After about two years there, I decided to go through the ordination process of the Baptist church, so I went before the board with five others. This process was a lot different from the nondenominational process. Here, we had to answer questions about our faith and the Word of God. This panel would be the deciding counsel. I was the first minister. They asked how do I know I am saved? The Spirit of the Lord came upon me, and I began to worship right before the board. They, in turn, began to worship. There was not a dry eye in the place. Once I was able to speak, I answered all the questions they asked, and they seemed shocked. They thanked me and said, "Many come before us and regurgitate the answers back to us, but today, we saw the evidence of your calling. The Holy Spirit showed up, and this became more than just a question-and-answer session." With tears flowing down my face, I thanked them for allowing the Holy Spirit to have His way in this place. I said, "God bless you!"

As I walked back into the main sanctuary where the other candidates were sitting, I tried to dry my tears, but they kept coming. They said, "We now understand what all the noise was. You were praising and worshipping God." One by one, each of them went back and returned, unsure of whether they had passed. When the last one returned, the board took a few minutes and then called each of us to sit at the table. Everyone passed, and they said, "Never had they seen that many candidates so well prepared." They congratulated us, and one of them said to me, "Thank you again!" I responded, "God bless!"

Before leaving, we were told by the head of the board that history was being made and that we needed to count ourselves blessed. We looked at each other, not saying a word.

He went on to say, "It had not been long since women were not allowed to preach in the Baptist association churches of that region, and tonight, we have five and one male who will be ordained. He said awesome job, and know you made history today."

We all left the church that night amazed at what God had done. About a month later, the ordination service was held, and each candidate was given a couple of minutes to say something. We were told to include the ordination board out of respect. We went in alphabetical order, which gave me time to see what the others were going to do.

When it was my turn, I said, "I would like to thank my Lord and Savior for making all this possible by calling us. I thank my pastor, who worked tirelessly to ensure we were prepared. I also thank the ordaining board for taking the time to ensure we were qualified. I would like to thank my church family because it was you who we stood before in training. You guys really know how to love the hell out of someone. Finally, I would like to thank my family (mom, daughter, sister, and cousin), who did not understand the call but accepted it. It is you guys who sacrifice when the call takes precedence over anything happening back home. I love you guys, and thanks for being supportive even when I know you wanted me there with you."

I felt the anointing of God come upon me, and I realized my life had changed that day. I was now ordained in two denominations, and I felt the pull of God on my life. He began to speak to me about some of the things he was preparing me for. I was terrified. I begged and pleaded with God to let me do it my way. I wanted to do outreach and nothing else, but God said, "No." I was on my way to purpose. After the ceremony was over, I went out to dinner with family and friends to celebrate. However, in the back of my mind, I wondered what in the world I just did? I honestly went along with the ordination to experience everything my co-laborers would. We were a team. However, God was going to hold me accountable for everything I experienced and learned. My journey had started, and I was not prepared for what was headed my way.

It didn't take long for my pastor to recognize the gifts. The problem was I hadn't. I remember a conversation between him and me one day.

He said, "You are one of the most important people at the church right now."

I said, "I'm not here for that; I just want to heal and learn more about God."

He said, "That's good, but I can see that you have a calling on your life that appears to be higher than the others."

At that moment, he called me "Apostle." I didn't verbally respond, but my eyes said it all. At that moment, I remembered the prophetess saying, "It is time that you stop dumbing down and walk fully in what God has called you to. God has called you to walk in all five of the five-fold ministry."

Now, I'm not going to tell you that this was the first time I had heard this because it's not. God had spoken this to me months before, and now my pastor was confirming it for the third time.

I knew in my heart that God was calling me, but I just wasn't sure how, when, or where. I wanted God to be pleased with me, so I was not going to move without God's approval. The truth is I may have been licensed in two denominations, but I didn't feel any different in that sense. I gained the title but still felt bound. I had no joy and no peace; I didn't trust people and, to be honest, didn't like them much either. Life had been cruel, and I was licensed and ordained to minister to people. I DIDN'T EVEN LIKE PEOPLE IN GENERAL BECAUSE OF ALL I HAD BEEN THROUGH, and now I'm called to minister to them. I didn't know a lot about the people of this particular church, so I attended but really wasn't a part of it.

I was saved but needed to be delivered from all of the things that had happened to me over the years. It was here that I would get my deliverance. I wish I could say it was pretty, but nope, it was ugly and painful as hell. Yep, that's what I said: painful as hell. This is how it all went down.

My pastor was awesome! He was a man who wanted each of us to understand why we were doing what we were doing at the time we were doing it. For instance, the question came up about why we stand at the head of the body when doing a committal. All kinds of answers came out. I answered by saying, "God conquered death and the grave; therefore, we stand at the head to indicate God being over death and the grave." Turns out there is no biblical reference in the Word about it. It had been adopted as a tradition that we simply started to follow. He also made us write papers on different topics. We preached, taught Bible studies, etc., just to name a few things. I was being challenged and stretched, to be honest it was like going to a second college. However, I felt an excitement because I was learning things I never knew.

Everything was going fine until it wasn't, if you know what I mean. I really wanted to be a part of the team, but I learned quick that I wasn't. There was a minister named Tiffany who told me no one was ever going to accept me because I wasn't one of them.

I said, "One of whom?"

She said, "Family!"

I said, "Really? I thought the only family that mattered was the one of Jesus Christ."

She smiled at me, never responding. The truth is there were originally four other women on the ministry team at this time and one male; can you say drama.

I spoke with my pastor about what was going on, and he said, "I believe God placed you here to pull them all together as a ministry team."

I said, "I don't think so."

You see everyone seemed to have beef with everyone. It was a headache. I shook my head in unbelief and said, "You have your hands full with this group." Now, I want you to understand I was not their leader. I was one of them; however, my pastor wanted to see who would emerge as the leader of the group.

So, my pastor started us meeting once a week in hopes that we would get to know each other and learn to respect our differences. I wish I could say it worked. The truth is my pastor was looking for an Assistant Pastor, and that position was like blood in the water, and the sharks were circling. It put everyone at odds with each other, or so it looked. They didn't know, but I had already talked to the pastor and asked him to pick the man because the women at that point was so full of drama. In my opinion, Wally was more prepared than any of us.

I remember speaking to him and telling him, "God is choosing you for the assistant Pastor position."

He said, "No, I think pastor is going to give it to you."

I said nope. I already talked to him. I'm not interested, and it's going to be you."

Two weeks later, he was named acting assistant pastor. You would think this would have made things better. Nope!

I remember a meeting where we all sat around a table and introduced ourselves, sharing a little of our backgrounds. I remember telling them that my heart's desire was to see my family saved, healed, and delivered so God would send me back home to minister and be an example of what I believed Him for. I told them it would take so much out of me that I would cry as I drove all the way home. I remember being so drained that I would just sleep for days.

One of them looked at me and said, "Then you're stupid. Why would you continually put yourself through this."

The tears began to run down my face, and I responded, "I don't want my family to go to hell, and if God tells me to do it in time, I will see what I have been praying for."

That same minister said, "I've been watching you, and you're either extremely happy or you're extremely sad. There is no middle ground with you."

The others agreed, and the line was drawn in the sand that day, and I was on one side all alone.

I was still okay with that because, to be honest, I wasn't looking for friends; I was looking for Jesus. I learned a few churches ago that this type of stuff goes on in leadership, and therefore, I wasn't shocked; in fact, I was looking for it. I had already been warned that I was not a part of the team because I was an outsider to them.

Now, truthfully, I wanted them to prove me wrong. I wanted them to prove that all these women could work together because it was God who called us to the table to serve in this ministry.

I remember one day, our pastor was praying for people, and the Lord spoke to me and said, "Have the ministers stand around the pastor to separate him from the congregation, which would minimize the warfare. You all will be his shield. God said to pray as he prays!" I spoke to the minister (Tiffany), who had been there the longest, trying to show her some respect. She ignored me! So, I blew it off and just figured she couldn't hear me with everything that was going on. I went to her after the service and repeated what God had said.

She put her finger in my face and said, "I heard you, but I am going to protect my pastor."

I said, "From who?"

"She looked at me and walked away.

Now, what's funny is this was the same woman I served with at the other church. In fact, I was the one who told her years earlier she was going to be going back to her home church. She was also the same woman that I took on a five-day cruise with me when I got my lump sum for disability. She was also the woman I took out to eat when she didn't have any money. She was also the same woman who went to the pastor and told him everything I had been doing at the other church. So why the hell did she feel the pastor needed protection from me? I immediately grabbed my things and left the church because I could not contain what I was feeling.

My anger went to rage, and I was ready to beat her behind, and I'm being nice. I started down the road and went back to beat the hell out of her when someone intervened and began to talk to me, which took my mind off it.

I don't know if the young lady knew what was going down or whether it was simply God's intervention. My witness would have been gone that day! I took a deep breath, answered the ladies' questions, and went home.

The ride home seemed very long because I was mad and fed up with being mistreated by church folks. However, I wanted to try to make things work at this church because I liked what my pastor was doing in training us. In the days, weeks, and months to come, things became more and more tense.

The pastor called a meeting with the ministers. He addressed the tension that was visible to him and to others. He said, 'There is tension between all of you," but it was especially bad between Tiffany and I. He gave a scenario of someone having an issue with someone in leadership and asked how we would handle it. Everyone around the table responded except me. I felt the anger rising back up inside me, so I decided not to say anything because I didn't want to disrespect him as my leader.

He said, "Minister Ann, I need an answer from you.

I said, "I choose not to answer."

He said, "We would not be leaving until you do. It is time for this thing to come out into the open."

I said, "This is not a good idea; just leave it alone."

He insisted.

I said, "I'm not playing these games."

Tiffany began to say, "See, pastor, this is how she is all the time!"

I yelled, "Shut up!" I hit the table as hard as I could, and I yelled, "Shut up. You know what you are doing."

Everything on the table began to fall, and everyone at the table jumped.

I looked at my pastor and said, "You don't know what goes on when you're not here, and I'm done taking it."

He said, "Really? You made a statement; now, finish it."

I said, "No, ask her."

Tiffany dropped her head and didn't say anything. Pastor said, "There's more going on here than I realize, and this has to stop." I didn't respond, and neither did Tiffany. He dismissed the meeting, and we went to service. The tension was unbelievable. However, I went and took a seat in the congregation and left them to the pulpit.

The next day, my pastor called and said, "You made a statement now tell me what you meant. What's going on that I don't know about in my church?"

I explained it all!

He said, "I will deal with her, but I'm sitting you down because you are furious and unable to deal with it properly."

I said, "Fine!"

About two weeks later, the pastor was absent from church, and Tiffany was in charge. The Spirit of the

Lord was moving in the service, and I began to sing. Tiffany from the pulpit shut it down. I then asked a deacon if I could get the bylaws of the church, and he said, "Yes." Tiffany stopped the service to ask the deacon what I wanted. He told her; she nodded and went back to doing the order of service.

My pastor called me a couple of days later, saying, "I was told that you wanted the by-laws of the church."

I said, "Yes."

He said, "Is there a specific reason why?"

I said, "Because I never received them when I joined."

He said, "OK, I will give permission for you to get them."

The strange thing about this is that, first, he was on a cruise, and second, someone contacted him about something I was supposed to get when I joined. Seems strange to me. Can you say red flag. This was only the beginning. Tiffany made sure I wasn't accepted in almost every area she could.

I remember an incident after being reinstated. I was teaching a Sunday school lesson. We were in Genesis talking about the Garden of Eden and how Adam and Eve disobeyed God. Someone brought up the concept of free will, that everyone has been given free will. I explained to the congregation that God never intended for us to choose anything outside of His will. I said, "We all have used the saying, "God gives us free will," but the truth is God said, "You can eat from this tree and that tree, but do not eat from this one." (paraphrasing) We were never supposed to know evil.

It was Satan who introduced that tree as an option. He went on to tell Eve God knows that you will surely not die but instead will know good and evil just as He does. The woman chose to believe Satan and ate the fruit and then convinced her husband to eat, which caused them to be cursed and kicked out of the garden. God never intended for us to experience all the things we experience in life today. Those things that break our hearts and destroy our bodies. That wasn't God's plan; it was Satan's.

So, after explaining it to the congregation and leaders, they opposed it. I said, "I will show it to you in the Word." I asked them to go to the passage and let's read it together.

Genesis 2:16 which states, "And the LORD God commanded him, "You may eat freely from every tree of the garden, but you must not eat from the tree of the knowledge of good and evil; for in the day that you eat of it, you will surely die."

Then Genesis 3:4-5 states, "You will not surely die," the serpent told her. 5"For God knows that in the day you eat of it, your eyes will be opened, and you will be like God, knowing good and evil."

Despite seeing it in the Bible for themselves, they still rebelled against the Word. I could not believe what I was hearing and seeing. So, I turned it over to the pastor to make a final decision. He stood up and said, "For twenty minutes, you have been fighting the truth even after it was shown to you in the Word. He said your hearts are hardened, and don't want to receive the truth because it's not what you're used to hearing." They all dropped their heads, including Tiffany, and I moved on with the study.

I want you to understand Tiffany was not the only person that had an issue with me. I bumped heads with deacons, other ministers, people on other auxiliaries, and the congregation. I don't think it was me personally; it was just the fact that I was not born and raised in that area, so it made me an outsider. For instance, there was a member whose husband passed. I was asked to teach the Bible study to the seniors on Tuesday at 12pm. Everything was fine until the day she came to me and said, "You don't teach like my husband, and I don't like it."

I told her I understood, but people have different teaching styles, and I must use the gifts God gave me. I spoke with my pastor, and he said continue. After a while, I was starting to get overwhelmed because I was still in school, helping a single mother out with her two children whom I had all the time, teaching Tuesday Bible study, attending minister meetings Tuesday evenings, going to Wednesday bible study, Sunday school, praise team rehearsal, and choir practice.

I went to the pastor with my concerns, telling him that I had spoken to another minister who was interested in helping on Tuesday. He gave his permission but said, "You are the lead on this ministry." I told him, 'There would be days I wouldn't get there, but Stacy would step in.'

He said, "That's fine, but I placed you over the ministry." I said, "I understand."

Long story short, I went to my pastor twice to give the ministry to Stacy so that she could run it and I could just assist her. Pastor said no both times!

He said, 'You're going to have to learn how to balance all the responsibilities of a pastor, so this would be good for me."

I took a deep breath and prepared for the next study. I can still remember that day because the tension was so bad; however, I opened the study and thanked Stacy for stepping in at the time of my absence. The members appeared to be confused based on the looks of their faces. However, I moved on. Stacy was finishing her series, but I noticed her topic was one-sided, so as I tried to introduce a different aspect of the text, she became arrogant and disrespectful. I let the first one slide. I noticed her and two of the ladies there whispering to which one was the lady whose husband had passed. Once I realized what was going on, I addressed it right then.

I said, "Despite going to the pastor twice to give this ministry to Stacy, he said no. So, I am the one over the study, and if you didn't like it, you can leave, and all of your followers can, too."

Their eyes got so big.

She said, 'What did you say?"

I said, "You heard me. Get out if there's a problem.

I don't think I made it home before my phone was ringing. Stacy called her bestie, who was also a minister at the church who, in turn, called the pastor. He said,

"Minister Ann, did you really tell them to get out of the church?" I said, "Yes."

He said, "How many times?"

I said, "Two or three."

He started laughing, saying, "Now you know better; you can't do that!"

I said, "Why? Jesus did. Did I not come to you twice about giving this Bible study to her?"

He said, "Yes, you did."

I said, "If it meant that much to her, why didn't she come to you or me? No, she went to the congregation. So, it is what it is."

He had the acting Assistant Pastor meet with us, and it only made things worse. His mind was already made up because they all were friends through the Baptist Association.

I was asked to apologize to the members of the Bible study, which I agreed to do. He instructed me to work with Stacy concerning the Bible study.

I said, "No, I'm not doing it. I am going to need you not to call my phone anymore."

He said, "What?"

"You heard me," I said.

My pastor called, and I repeated everything I told the assistant.

He said, "Well, he is going to call you."

I said, "Well, he will talk to my voicemail because I won't be answering."

I was once again sat down for two weeks. I said, "Nope, I'm afraid it's going to take a while this time. I said we can start at a month and see how it goes."

At this point, I was more content with sitting down. I knew that God was doing something in me, but it was painful when all I wanted to do was serve Him. I was learning the difference between serving God and serving man. I was wrong in the eyes of man a lot, but God was pleased. So, my focus became more and more focused on God, and I cared less about what man thought.

My pastor tried to keep me engaged. For instance, the ministers went to a Baptist convention. He messed with me the entire time because I was quiet and didn't try to take part. He would make comments like, "You're going to talk this week" and "What do you need?" "How are you?" "What do you want to do tonight?" There were times we went out to eat, and the other ministers would sit around him, and I would sit on the end, away from everyone. He would move his plate down to where I was and try to include me in the conversation. Most times, I would say, "I have no opinion." He never gave up. I can't say for sure, but I think the others tried too hard, and I was the opposite; I didn't try at all. Let me give you an example: the ministers decided they were going to take the pastor out for his birthday one year. Well, he likes crab legs. I didn't want to go there because I don't eat them. I asked if everyone could afford this place because it was expensive, and I had heard some of them talking about their money was short. They all agreed, yes! However, when it was time to go, there was an issue because some didn't have the money. They ended up using church funds to pay the bill. So, I asked, "If you could not afford it, why didn't you ask to go to a less expensive place? So it wasn't from the minister but the church?" We were then told that the pastor shouldn't know about it. I said, "Oh, now we are keeping secrets from the pastor." They moved on to the next topic.

I saw things of that nature starting to happen more and more. It would be to the point of putting a financial strain on the people, trying to please the pastor. Everything was about the pastor, and I was hearing less and less about what God wanted. The thing is, I never heard the pastor ask for these things. It was all happening to impress the pastor for a position that had already been filled. I think the problem was that an acting assistant pastor had been chosen but was not going to fill the position permanently. So, in their minds, I guess they felt they still had a shot, and they were willing to do whatever was necessary to get it. Truthfully, there is nothing wrong with aspiring for something more; it's just how some of them went about getting it that bothered me.

Now, I want you to understand there were so many situations that took place that it is impossible to tell it all, so I want to skip to the one that did the most damage. There was a young man in the church that Tiffany liked. I knew and truthfully had tried to hook them up before I realized who Tiffany really was. She tried everything to get close to him, but nothing seemed to work. I noticed that everyone, including our pastor, was trying to fix them up, but he still wasn't responding the way she wanted him to. So, she eventually came back to me and said he wasn't interested. However, she secretly still desired him.

One day, while speaking to a prophetess, she said she had a word from the Lord for me.

I asked her what it was, and she began to say these words, "There is a man in your church who likes you. He will be your husband. However, another woman likes him, and he knows it, but he is not interested in her. He wants you." She went on to say, "You have even tried to hook them up, but he is not interested. He respects her as a minister but doesn't like her the way she likes him."

I said, "I know who you are talking about, but she was my friend at one time, and I can't and won't do her that way."

She said, "Oh, so what she wants is more important than what God wants? This is a God thing; you guys have a ministry to do together. Besides, this is the man you prayed for."

I said, "What do you mean?"

She said, "You prayed and asked God to send you a husband who knows the Word and could teach you. You prayed for someone you could talk to about anything. You prayed for someone familiar with music, and he plays an instrument. You asked for someone that was pleasing to your eyes, and he is, and you asked for someone you wouldn't get bored with sexually."

I was in awe because I never spoke to anyone about what I prayed for concerning what I wanted in a husband, so I knew this had to be a God moment. She was right, I did. But this was the first time I had thought of that prayer in years, and besides, how could I do that to a friend. I thanked her for the word and went about my way, floored at how precise she was.

About two months later, I saw Terrell on Facebook. He had made a comment saying he had a lot on his mind. I don't know why I responded, but I did.

I said, "I know how you feel. Call me if you need someone to talk to. Check your inbox."

I left my number and said, "I'm not on FB much, but you can call if you want to."

He replied with his number and mentioned he was not on Facebook much, either.

We didn't talk again for another month or so, though I saw him in church every week.

Terrell was in his early sixties and about 6ft tall. He was light-skinned. He wasn't fat but was a nice size. His hair was neatly cut, and he had no facial hair. And he always smelled so good. That man could play that guitar like nobody's business. He was definitely easy on the eyes. I see why Tiffany liked him.

Terrell finally called after a while, and we hit it off great. The prophetess was right; we could talk about any and everything. There were many days that we talked from one state right into the next one. You see, Terrell was a truck driver, so talking helped him out. We found out so much about each other, and we never ran out of things to say. I felt like I had known him all my life, and before I knew it, I was developing feelings for him and had never met him outside of the church.

One day, Terrell said, "I'm getting ready to pull into my yard, and I want to know if it is too late to meet me."

I said, "No? Where?"

He gave me the directions and time, and I was off. We ended up meeting at a school just a little before dark. He asked if he could kiss me, and I said, "Yes," but quickly pushed him away. I immediately thought, "I know this man didn't get me to come out here for some hanky panky!"

He wanted to know why I pushed him away, and I said, "You're pretty good at that."

He said, "You are too!"

I said that's why I pushed you away!"

We both laughed, and I got into his car. He said, "I wanted to at least have that to remember you by if our conversation doesn't go well."

I said, "OK, what's up?"

He went on to tell me that Tiffany likes him, but he has never been interested in her.

I said, "Well, I kind of figured that because she told me that you wouldn't go out with her."

He said, "No. I respect her as a minister but am not interested in a relationship with her. He went on to say, it has been you since the day you walked into the church. You're the one I want. However, I don't want to cause confusion in the church because I work there."

I said, "I understand."

He said, "I need you to know I'm not going to stop talking to her on the phone.

"Since we are having this conversation, I need to know out of your mouth. Are you interested in her?" I asked.

"No!" he responded.

"Have you ever gone out with her?"

"No!" he responded.

"Are you leading her on in any way?"

"No!" he responded.

I said, "If we choose to pursue this, are you the type of man to deal with two women out of the same pulpit?"

"No, Ann!" he responded.

I said, "Then we understand each other. I know that she likes you; however, we are two adults in agreement about what we want to do. That's all that matters!"

He said, "Now that it's out of the way. Why do you sometimes seem close to me and other times pull away?"

I said, "I wanted to talk to you about that."

"What's up?" he said.

I went on to tell him about everything I had gone through with Bobby and how I lost my baby behind a bunch of lies.

I said, "Terrell, listen, I can't handle lies. We are both adults, and I need you to be straight up with me. I may not like what you say, but I will respect the fact that you told me the truth. To me, lies are like rape. I need the truth so I can make the best decision for me, and I can only do that if I know what's up."

"I understand," he said.

By this time, the rain and wind started to get heavy, and the mood changed. Before I knew it, we were kissing again, but this time, I didn't pull away. Things got really heated, and before I knew it, we were in the back seat, and things started happening. You know, grown-up stuff. His kisses tasted like strawberry, and his touch was tender and endearing. I was lost in the moment when I heard him whisper, "Are you okay?" I whispered, "Yes," and for the first time in my life, I knew what it was like for a man to truly make love to me. You see, I thought I knew, but no, I didn't. I had never in my life experienced anything like this before. I was 48 years old and making love for the first time in the backseat of a car. It was raining, and the wind was blowing! It was like a scene from a movie. I think both of us were shocked that this happened at all, but I was shocked that it happened in his car.

In that moment, I fell in love with this man. I know it sounds crazy, but everything I prayed and asked God for was right in front of me. My mind knew that we had only been communicating a short while, but my heart and Spirit had known him all my life. We both needed time to process what just happened, so we kissed good night, and he backed his car up so that I could get into mine without getting wet.

Terrell stayed on the phone with me until I got almost home. I told him, "I'm almost home, and you need to go to sleep, seeing how you have an early run the next morning."

He hesitantly agreed.

Once he hung up, the radio came on, and I heard that there was a tornado in our area, which was why there was so much wind and rain.

I said, "OMG, he and I both could be dead right now. Lord, please forgive me and protect me to get home safely." I pulled into my yard five minutes later. I said, "Thank you, Jesus."

I remember going into the house and sitting on the side of the bed, thinking about what had just happened. It was the sweetest, most tender moment I ever experienced in my life. After showering, I said my prayers and turned over to go to sleep. The phone rang, and Terrell wanted to know if I was home.

I said, "Yes, I just got in bed."

We both said good night and planned to talk again the next day. I fell asleep with a smile on my face and in my heart. Something I had not done in quite a long time.

Terrell and I continued to talk on the phone for another two weeks when we both decided it was time we met under "normal" circumstances. It seems both of us were thinking the same thing but never said a word until it was over.

I remember him looking at me, saying, "Wow, it was better than before. The other time seemed more like a movie scene, and so, I wanted to be with you under normal circumstances."

I couldn't believe I was hearing this from him because I felt the same way. I was just too embarrassed to say it.

My mind was blown because Terrell was an older man. He knew what he needed and wanted, and he was very interested in every aspect of my life. He didn't seem to mind all the terrible decisions I'd made along the way. In fact, we often talked about how certain decisions shaped us and brought us to where we were at that time. We talked about our accomplishments and our biggest regrets. I loved being with this man in every way because he gave me things to think about but also respected our differences. He simply let me be me without trying to change me, and I did the same.

I remember one day, he was talking about how he felt when his wife asked him to leave home. He never got over the hurt of not being in the home to raise his babies.

He said, "Ann, it still hurts today, and they're almost thirty. I couldn't be the dad they needed because I wasn't in the house with them, and I will never forgive her for that."

I was speechless!

Then, out of the blue, he said, "If or when we have babies, and I'm disciplining them, wait until we are in the room before trying to talk to me."

I said to myself, "Wait a minute. We don't have any babies, and I'm not trying to."

He then said, "Ann, I'm holding back tears right now."

I said, "I know, I can hear them."

He said, ‘I will never get those days back with my boys.” I said, “Terrell, I’m sorry that you’re hurting, and I pray God heals you.”

A silence came over the line, and he then said. “I need to call you back. I have to drop this load.”

I said, “Okay,” and as I hung up the phone, I could feel the tears running down my face. He was too proud to cry, so I did for him. I asked God that day if he could use me to heal him of all his hurt and pain, as I was willing.

Approximately six weeks later, I started to feel nauseous. I couldn’t shake it. I talked to my girlfriend Monique after a few weeks, who said I think you may be pregnant. I said no, “I think it’s the flu or something. I told her I was going to give it a few more days, and if it didn’t get better with the over-the-counter medicine, I would go in to see the doctor.”

About another week passed, and the symptoms were the same. I made an appointment with my regular doctor, who did a urine test. Negative! I was so happy because I was finally enjoying life, and I didn’t want any more responsibility. My doctor told me to continue the over-the-counter medication, and it should pass in a couple of days.

Another week passed, and I wasn’t feeling any better. So, Monique made an observation; she said, “You are only sick from early morning to 12 or 1 p.m., and then you’re perfectly fine. Then it starts over again the next morning, and you’ve been doing this for quite a while.”

I said, "I have been to the doctor, and the test was negative."

She said, "I think you should make one with your OBGYN."

I got an appointment the following week. While there, I took a urine test that came back negative, but the ultrasound found a pregnancy. However, I was told the embryo wouldn't survive because the sac had not formed around it. The NP pushed for me to abort the pregnancy. I said, "No, I couldn't make a decision without Terrell." I was in shock. How did this happen? I mean, we were always so careful. God reminded me of the day Terrell kept asking me if he had to pull out. He must've asked 3 to 4 times, and I looked at him and finally said, "Yes, we don't want any children."

I became so angry because I felt like he set me up. Monique quickly reminded me of the prayer I told her I prayed about healing him. I calmed down, took a deep breath, and called Terrell.

Terrell became angry with me because I brought up aborting the baby. I said listen, "I'm only telling you what the nurse said. The decision is not mine alone." He said, "If you don't want it, I will raise it."

My tears became too much for me to contain, and I said, OKAY, Terrell, I will talk to you later."

I was confused.

Terrell called me right back and said, "If the baby isn't going to live, that's God's decision, but please don't abort it. Ann, you're a big girl, and no one will know that you're pregnant."

I agreed to let God be God.

He said, "I will take care of my baby because I know what it's like to feel thrown away like no one cares."

My mind went back to what he said concerning his childhood, and I couldn't get rid of his baby. He was right; no one knew the difference, probably because we were gearing up for the pastor's anniversary, not to mention I was a big girl, as he put it.

Now, Tiffany had no idea what was going on, but I heard God say three times to tell her.

I said, "Tell who what God?"

He said, "Tell Tiffany about your relationship with Terrell."

I said, "No, this cannot be God because this will certainly cause more tension in the church." I closed my eyes and said, "God, if this is you, have her call me, and I will tell her."

Well, it took about two months, and sure enough, Tiffany called and came straight out and asked about Terrell and me. I confirmed what she thought. I went on to tell her that he said he had a lot of respect for her but was not interested in her in that way.

I said, "He told me that's why your conversation never went any further than talking about the Bible."

She got quiet.

I said, "We have been seeing each other for a little over two years but recently stopped because the calling became more important."

She said, "I wouldn't have been able to stop, not even for the call."

"How is he?" she said.

"What do you mean?" I asked.

She said, "I have dreamed of what it would be like to be with him."

I said, "All I am willing to say is that he is a nice guy who happens to have a calling on his life.

She said, "Well, can I pray about anything?"

I said, "Not really, but if you feel the need to pray for him, pray that he becomes everything God has ordained for his life."

She then asked if she could say a prayer. Her prayer started with, "Please forgive me, God, for wanting something I couldn't have." Then, she went on to pray for Terrell. She thanked me for being honest, and we hung up.

Terrell and I continued as friends after having a conversation about me being true to my calling. Terrell wanted me to walk worthy of my call. He didn't want to be the reason I sinned against God. It was an adjustment, but I loved him, and the truth is he was right. So, we talked from time to time instead of all the time like we used to.

Months passed when, one day, I tried to get in contact with Terrell, and he wouldn't answer my call. I knew something had gone wrong but had no clue as to what it was. I made up my mind that I would try one more time, and if he didn't answer, I was done.

Terrell answered, "Why did you talk to someone about me?"

"I am clueless as to what you are talking about," I said.

"I know you did, Ann, he came to me. You don't understand that I know a lot of people."

"Ok, who said it, and what did I supposedly say so we can deal with it face to face?"

"I'm not going to tell you," he said

"Wow. I learned quickly that my words no longer mean anything to you. I didn't speak to any man about us. However, I have had people come to me about why you stare so hard at me in church, but I never brought it to you because this was never about them; it was about us. But, at least, I now understand why you went quiet on me. Goodbye!"

One day, while praying, I heard the voice of God say Tiffany went to the pastor about your relationship with Terrell. The following Sunday, I went to church and respectfully confronted my pastor, and he confirmed it. He said he handled it and that I should not be concerned. I tried to carry on, but deep down, I was mad as hell.

The pastor's Anniversary was all scheduled when the Lord spoke to me and said I would not be participating this year.

I said, "Why, God?"

He said, "I will not allow you to put on a show before the people as though you are a team when, in fact, behind closed doors, you don't get along."

I was shocked. However, I needed to tell the other ministers. I immediately called the Assistant Pastor, explaining what God had said to me.

He asked, "What is the pastor going to think?"

I said, "I don't care. God told me no!"

When that Tuesday came, the Assistant Pastor said, "Minister Ann has something she needs to tell us."

I explained what God had said, "He is not allowing me to participate in the Pastor's Anniversary because if we are not a team behind closed doors, I won't pretend to be one in front of the people."

Each Minister went around the table giving their opinions. There were comments like, "Why can't you go along with what everyone else is doing?" Why do you have to be so different?" and "Anytime she thinks she's heard God, she's not going to budge."

"Her mind is made up," one of them said.

I said, "You're right. I am not going to budge when I know what God said to me."

Then another minister asked, "Well, what does that mean for us?"

I said, "Nothing. I just can't participate!

Finally, the meeting was dismissed, and I headed home. I was later told by Tiffany that they had another meeting about me after I left.

I responded, "Really, I'm not surprised at all."

We suddenly started hearing about people getting sick; the hospitals were full, and people were dying at an alarming rate. I'm talking about people all over the world. Pastor decided to close the doors of the church because there just wasn't enough information about this virus. Covid 19 was running rampant, and people were terrified. My pastor decided that we could no longer meet face to face, so I instructed all the ministers to come together by phone through calls or Duo to pray for the world and the effects the virus was having on it. However, the calls became so intense that I could no longer be a part of it. I mean, while on Duo, there was rolling of eyes, ministers not speaking to other ministers, one minister turned and faced the wall to keep from being seen. I knew that those prayers couldn't be getting to God, not with all the confusion that was going on. I sent a message to all the ministers and my pastor, informing them that I would no longer be a part of leadership at the church. I told them that God had not moved me from the church, so I would continue my membership with the Assistant Pastor as my minister. My Pastor called, and I confirmed my intentions.

The Pastor's Anniversary was canceled and never rescheduled due to the pandemic, as there was no end in sight. Although God told me I wouldn't be participating, I just didn't know He was going to shut down the world. I started spending a lot more time in prayer, and what God was showing me blew my mind. He said, "The people are being sifted." You see, the ministers seemed to care more about the pastor than they did about God.

It was always more, and the members couldn't afford it. However, I had sold tickets to the Pastor's Anniversary to friends of mine. The Lord instructed me to ask them if they wanted their money back.

He said, "Pay it out of your pocket instead of asking the church to refund it. The Lord said that people would begin to say that the pastor and the church stole their money. So, offer to refund it."

I inwardly agreed and began to make the necessary phone calls. However, one of the people I sold the tickets to (the pastor who took my license) didn't respond to me but called my pastor and asked why he was refunding money to the people. He said, "They were donations.

By this time, my pastor had started a live Facebook stream to minister to the people. He literally went off yelling that the money was his and his wife's and that no one was getting their money back. He then started talking about me in every message he preached. This went on for about 6 months! He said things like, "You're weak, and that's why you sat down. You're simply not cut out to handle the pressure of being called. You left the ministry because you couldn't have the man you wanted." He then looked at Terrell and said, "Ain't that right?" Of course, Terrell responded, "That's right, pastor!"

My anger quickly turned to rage, and I started dreaming about shooting up the church. The Lord spoke and said, "Do not return to the church until I tell you to, and do not watch any more of his services."

God gave me two other pastors to watch online—Pastor John Gray and TD Jakes. I watched every service that I could find, and they all applied to my life. So, God was still ministering to me. I found myself studying, praying, and fasting all day. I continued my praise and worship right here in my house.

One day, while sitting on the side of my bed, I said, "God, I'm tired, and if this is all there is to ministry and life, I want to go home and be with you." I said, "Change me, God. That way, I can handle the people that come my way."

My prayer had been before to change the people, but I realized that I would have to pray that prayer over and over again based on the people I met.

God said, "You finally got it. You mean it this time. Now give me your mind, will, and emotions."

I'm not going to lie to you that things changed overnight because they didn't. In fact, the truth is my circumstances seem to be worse, but I was committed and submitted to God's process concerning my life. I was tired and knew that there was nothing I could do on my own. I was completely dependent on God.

Before you know it, months had passed, and the pastor was opening the church up for outside services. He continued to livestream on Facebook as a second option for people to get the Word. However, rumors were growing just as God said they would. Phone calls started coming into the members who wanted to know why the pastor was acting the way he was online. When they came to me, I told them that I was no longer part of the leadership and, therefore, they needed to speak with someone who could answer their question. For me, I was waiting for God to release me from the ministry because I was done. God had started a work in me, and I wasn't giving up the progress I had made.

Soon, God allowed me to start watching the services again, and it was more of the same, but at least, this time, I wasn't the only one being bashed. It was different this time because I had no response. There was no anger, and my heart was to pray for him and all the ministers who supported him in this manner. The moment I began to pray for him, I heard God say, "Now I can deal with them for what they did."

I said, "God, it is not necessary!"

The Lord said, "Be quiet because this is not about you. My Word says touch not my anointed and do my prophet no harm. I'm obligated to vindicate you. Everything I promised you will come to pass. I'm going to use everything that happened to show them that I am God, and I will expose the hearts of my people to bring them to a place of repentance. You obeyed me, and heaven backs you. Start attending the services, but remain quiet and watch me change things."

I agreed and did as God instructed by attending the services but not taking part in leadership.

I started doing outreach, helping at the church's food pantry until it was stopped. I also had an outreach that I started years ago. It was nothing major, just me helping people as my income would allow. My heart was to help as many people as I could because the pandemic was brutal to many. Therefore, I prayed and said, "God, how can I help your people?" He instructed me to use my credit card and renew my loans and that He would foot the bill. If there was a need and God pointed me to someone, I gave. I trusted God to do exactly what He said he would. God had me doing the opposite of what the world was doing. The world was stockpiling supplies, and here I was, taking money and sowing it into the lives of God's people. I didn't have anything extra, and God took care of me, I believe because I took care of His people.

My life was slowly but surely changing for the better because I now had a better understanding of who God was to me. It had become personal, and I realized that my mother's faith wasn't enough for me. Don't get me wrong; it was a start, but I desired so much more. I realized that everything I had been through was to bring me to that day when I said, "Enough, God, something has got to change." The change started that day in me. I still have a long way to go, but I thank God for the progress. I know I can do this because God is truly with me.

Looking back, I see myself as many Christians are today. I had a form of godliness but denied the power thereof. Chapter 7 was my convergence into the true revelation of who God was to me. I had a form of Godliness but was denying the power of God to truly change me. I didn't have to be like everyone else. I was what I was seeing in other people. I wasn't different, but I expected everyone else to be different. I wondered why married men kept showing up in my life until the day I sat down and listened to stories my mom told me. It's in our bloodline. It was simply generational, and I wanted to break the cycle. No matter how hard I tried to stay away from these married men, they always seemed to sneak in, and I would break it off once I found out.

I've learned that the Word of God is true, and it's there to protect us from these very situations. If I had not been having sex, then none of these situations would have happened, and my life wouldn't have gotten so far off track.

The second thing I want to address is that church people are not necessarily Christ-centered people. I learned quickly that though we say we served the same God, the church became the most controversial part of my life. People tend to want to control you or your gifts, and if you don't comply, they talk about you turning people against you. The infamous clique every church has. I would be speaking the Word, and it would still be rejected because it was me saying it. How can I speak about God but live a worldly life? No power or authority. No change. However, for once, I came to a place where I was tired and wanted a real relationship with God. Satisfying the desire of man was history, and I was pressing and reaching for something greater in God. It was all or nothing for me at this point. I literally had nothing else to lose. It was time for a change.

I had to learn that though my pastor recognized my gifts, I needed to be healed. I believe he had good intentions, and he only did to me what was done to him. The problem was I was called to something different, and because of that, I began to see certain aspects of the training as abuse, and I simply wasn't doing it anymore. I had enough God in me to walk away and get the healing I needed right inside my own house. Are you willing to walk away from anything and everybody to get the healing you may desperately need?

To some, you may say that I stayed in this mode for a long time, but I'm here to tell you that it takes some people a long time to get out of destructive cycles. I remember the woman in the Bible that had an issue of blood. I, like her, had tried everything, almost losing everything we had. She stayed in that situation for 12 years before she had a revelation. That revelation pushed her to break tradition and customs to get her breakthrough. What are you willing to push through to get your breakthrough?

Reflection

As I look back, I asked myself what was going on with me? I was a dysfunctional, carnal Christian. I had no idea that the molestation and rape had caused a ripple effect and that a lust demon was at work unknowingly in my life. However, God allowed all of these things to happen as they did so that I would desire and search for a deeper relationship with Him. I don't believe it was God punishing me for not following His Word. I believe it was the consequences of my actions that I was reaping. Though I did not start this vicious cycle as a child, my bad decisions as an adult led me to this place. I've learned now that if the Bible says it's wrong, then just don't do it; It's not worth it.

The cost was high. It cost me my self-esteem, the love I had for myself, my peace, and my joy. I begged God for death, but instead, He gave me life through His sacrifice. Grace and mercy showed up, restoring all that I had lost. He is no longer just Savior but Lord and deliverer. He has become my everything! My life was jacked up, but God resurrected me. Now, I offer people the same, pointing people to the one who can resurrect them.

Choose God by learning His nature and allowing the power of the Holy Spirit to change you from the inside out. Don't look out and around at others comparing your walk to others. Instead, look up in submission to Him and him alone. You will be glad you did!

CHAPTER EIGHT

The 8th Hour: The Proverbs 31 Woman

I continued to stay in the Word of God despite what was going on at church. Everything I did seemed to bother someone. If I sang, they complained I was singing too loud. If I taught Bible study, they complained, and if I preached a Word, they complained. I think the very breath I breathed bothered them. So, I finally decided that God had been too good to me to allow anyone or anything to steal my praise. I had finally put the drama behind me, and I was doing what I was created to do.

One day, while I was sitting in in-person service, I heard the Lord say look up. I looked right into Terrell's eyes. Evidently, he had been watching me, and I immediately got angry. His eyes told it all! He still had feelings for me.

I prayed, saying, "God, I'm over it. He has his life, and I have mine. Besides, God, he literally told me he wishes I would drop f---ing dead!"

The Lord said, "He has a soul."

I said, "I'm not the one to help him. My voice means nothing to him anymore. He's not the man I fell in love with. So, I've moved on! God, please just let me serve you in peace. I don't need a husband, and to be honest, I don't want one, either. I've finally made it to this place in you, and I'm not giving it up."

He said, "Ann, you need a covering in these streets. It's dangerous."

I said, "No, God, not him. If you want me to have a husband, send someone else, just not him. I don't want my relationship with you to be affected because of my relationship with a man. I have been through that, and I'm not willing to lose you just to be married. I have made it to the secret place, and I'm not going back to all the arguing and the desire to be heard. I've accepted that marriage is not for me. "

God never responded.

I woke up the next morning, and I heard, "Study the Proverbs 31 woman."

I said, "God, I know the story, but I will study it."

Proverbs 31:10-11 (NIV) A wife of noble character who can find? She is worth far more than rubies. Her husband has full confidence in her and lacks nothing of value.

As I studied this woman, I thought, This is an amazing woman who loves the Lord and provides for her family. She also has the love and respect of her family, and she strives at making them first despite all she must do. This woman knows who she is, and she knows her purpose and doesn't seem to struggle with it. I would love to be this type of woman. No matter how hard I try, I always seem to fall short. It seems unattainable. I will make a pact with you, God; I will marry the man of your choosing, but this time you have to do it. I have tried it on my own twice with the same outcome—divorce. The first time, I gave up because it wasn't getting any better. The second time, he gave up, and You, Lord, instructed me to leave because he grew more abusive daily. I have washed my hands on this thing called love, so if it is what you desire for me, you're going to have to show me your way. God, if this is your will, I want a Godly husband, as the scripture talks about. He must be a man who loves You with all His heart, mind, and soul. Then, just maybe, he will know how to love me. Nothing else will do!

I studied that scripture off and on for months. However, it soon faded into the background because there was no one I was interested in or who was interested in me. I became complacent once again with going to church and working my outreach. One day, a pastor contacted me on Facebook. He said he was interested in me coming to his church to do a service. He explained that he was starting a ministry and that he thought that I would be a good fit for an opening service. He said he had been watching me on Facebook and liked what he saw. I immediately went to his page to see if this was legitimate. Everything seemed to check out, so I dropped my number in his inbox and told him to call me whenever he had everything set up to discuss the details. In about five minutes, he called.

The moment I heard his voice, I knew I had talked to him before. A few years earlier, a mutual friend introduced me to him, but he became too aggressive for me. I hadn't heard from him in several years. Tyrone had been ministering for quite a while and had sung with a famous local group.

He said, "I know that God has called me to Pastor, but due to certain circumstances, I got sidetracked." He went on to ask, "Are you seeing someone?"

I said, "No, and I'm not looking for any type of relationship at this time."

He said, "I know what that means; you've been hurt.'

I said, "Yes, but I just want to focus on my outreach ministry right now. I'm in a good place with God, and I am not interested in any more drama."

He said, "Well, I understand that."

He wanted to know about my outreach and what I felt God was calling me to do. He then told me the same. He wants to pastor a church and open a funeral home. I applauded him for finally starting to do what he felt God was calling him to do. I then told him that I needed to go because I was in the middle of something, but call me when he got things together with his church.

That night, as I drifted off to sleep, I heard the Lord say, "You're going to have sex."

I said, "No, God, I will not sin against you. I'm over that stuff. That's not my life anymore."

The tears began to run down my face because the truth was, I had no desire to be with anyone. This wasn't the first time God had said something like this to me. I know that it wasn't His will for me to have sex, not being married, but more of a warning. God knows us better than we know ourselves. There was no one in my life that I desired in that way, so I didn't understand what God was saying. It troubled me greatly. Sex leads to heartbreak, and I wasn't completely healed yet from Terrell. I quickly dismissed what I heard, figuring the enemy was playing with me.

Before I knew it, morning had come, and Tyrone was calling. I answered, curious as to why he was once again calling so soon. I had made myself clear, but he wasn't getting it.

He said, "I don't believe in beating around the bush. I think you're the woman I have been praying for."

I said, "What do you mean?

He said, "I believe you're my wife, and I don't believe in long engagements. I took a deep breath but remained quiet."

He said, "Did you hear me? There are some things that we need to talk about, though. Things that you need to know about me."

I said, "I thought I told you that I wasn't interested. Besides, I haven't heard from you in years. Marriage? No! What happened to your wife?"

He said, "The marriage didn't work out, so we got divorced."

Now, this was crazy because he didn't know the conversation that I had had with God prior to him contacting me.

He said, 'Listen, can you pray about it to see what God has to say about it?"

I hesitantly agreed.

However, we started communicating every day several times a day, in fact. A couple of weeks had passed when he asked if he could come down to visit. He was eager to show me his plans for his church and funeral home and wanted my opinion on a few things. I honestly think he wanted to see if I believed in what he was trying to do. Tyrone seemed to know what he wanted, and he was finally able to move forward. And he wanted me to be a part of it all. I prayed about him coming, and the Lord said, "Yes, let him come; it's ministry."

He said, "How about this weekend?"

I agreed and said, "I need to go. I have some things I need to get done today."

We hung up, and I went on about my day.

Tyrone called me later that week on Duo. I could not believe it because he was naked and masturbating. I hung up! He called back, and I hung up again. When he called back, he said, "Listen, if you're going to be my lady, then this is what I like to do. I don't want to talk about church all the time."

I said, "I'm not, and don't call me again."

I then remembered that this was why I stopped talking to him before.

He said, "Ann, wait, I see that this bothers you, and I'm sorry, I won't do it again."

I said, "I know because we won't be on another video call."

He said, "I understand!"

I prayed again, "God, are you sure about him coming here?"

He said, "Yes, it's ministry."

I took a deep breath and said, "Okay."

Tyrone called me every day, I believe, to make sure I didn't change my mind about him coming.

I picked him up that Friday from the bus station, where he was still wearing his work clothes. He was about 5'7, dark-skinned with wavy short hair. Tyrone was a large build man but not fat. He said that he was exhausted from working all night and then riding for hours on the bus. He said all he wanted was to take a shower and go to bed. He did just that. I closed the door to let him rest peacefully. Besides, I still had other things I needed to get done before I focused on Tyrone.

After hours of sleep, he woke up hungry, so we decided to go out and pick something up. Tyrone had never been to this area before, so he was excited to look around and ask questions.

He said, “I think this would be a great place to start a ministry and business.”

I said, “Excuse me, you don’t live here.”

He said, “I could. I’m willing to move here if you would marry me.”

I said, “Are you still talking about that?”

He said, “Yes, because I know you are the one.”

Once we picked the food up, we headed back to my place so that we could talk. Tyrone had a lot on his mind, and he was determined to talk to me about it all today.

Once he finished eating, he said, “I need to tell you something.”

I asked, “What was it?

He said, ‘I went to prison for rape.”

I said, “Excuse me.”

He said, “Yes, I served one year. Before you say anything, let me explain.” He went on to say that he was a young kid who got coerced into a confession by the prosecutors. He said, “I was told that if I didn’t plead guilty, they would lock me up for a long time. I honestly didn’t know what to do, so I figured, what’s a year. I took the deal! After serving the year, I found out that they had no proof against me through the discovery. I was young and scared.”

He went on to tell me that he was trying to get the conviction overturned and that the prosecutor had already been terminated. It seems he had a regular practice of forcing confessions out of young black men. His story seemed plausible because I worked in law enforcement for about fifteen years, so I knew this type of thing happened a lot.

Tyrone said, "A lot happened to me while in prison. I don't remember a lot about what happened, but as a result, I now have a pacemaker."

He opened his shirt and showed me the surgery incision. He said," And I can no longer drive because of the violent seizures I have. He went on to say, my mom and dad were killed in a car accident on their way home from church on the same day."

I saw him spiritually shrink into a childlike posture while talking about his parents. He was deeply wounded because he was not able to attend their services to say goodbye.

He also said the conviction had strained his relationship with people in his family because they now look at him differently. He said, "And there is one more thing. I have a daughter that has been lost to the system. Her mother moved away to another city when she was a baby, and I lost track of her." She had been in the Department of Social Services for nine years, and he had finally found her. He said he was determined to get her out and build a relationship with her.

I took a deep breath and said, "Anything else?"

He said, "No, that's it?"

I said, "Thanks for sharing all of this."

He said, "Ann, I want us to build something together, and I need to be honest with you. I have a horrible label, and you will be affected by it as well. So, I need you to understand what you would be walking into if you said yes."

I said, "Tyrone, listen; my past is jacked up, too, but I trust God to work all these things out. I told him that he needed to do the same. This is what my outreach ministry is all about. I'm determined to let people know that God can turn things around. It doesn't matter what they said or did; God can change their lives if we are willing to let Him. I can't judge you."

He seemed relieved.

I said, "I must ask, did you do it?"

He said, "No." He went on to say that he was dating the pastor's daughter, and she wanted more than he was willing to give her. He said things had gotten bad between them, and the pastor wanted to know what was going on. Instead of owning up to the relationship, she lied and said he raped her. It definitely was plausible because a lot of the men in jail were there for that very reason. I accepted his response, unsure of what to think at that point.

As each of us prepared to go to bed that night, the conversation continued to flow, and we seemed to grow closer. My nervousness was gone, and Tyrone tapped into some things that I had been talking to God about. The tears began to run down my face because I knew that it had to be God speaking. The prophetic gift was flowing, and I stopped fighting because I knew this was a God thing. Tyrone was the answer to my prayers. How could he know these things? God had answered my prayers and sent another. I told Tyrone I needed to sleep because it had been a long day.

He said, "Can I hold you?"

I hesitantly said. "Yes."

As I started to fall asleep, I could feel Tyrone getting an erection. I didn't respond. He then started kissing on the back of my neck. I said, "Tyrone, no, I don't live like that anymore." I remembered what God said, "You're going to have sex." Tyrone said, "Ann, I love everything about you, and I want us to be together. I want you to be my wife."

I didn't respond but started to feel weak because it had been a while since I was with anyone. I finally gave in and slept with him. Afterward, I sat on the side of the bed, filled with guilt, not because of God but because I felt like I had betrayed Terrell. I couldn't contain my tears. Tyrone said, "Ann, you really weren't into it, were you?

I said, "No."

He said, "I need you to be straight with me. What's going on?"

I went into the whole spill about Terrell and how it affected me.

I told him, "I didn't move on because I wanted to but because I was forced to."

I explained how I felt the devil had stolen one more thing from me, and I was doing my best to make peace with it. On top of that, I was pregnant, which made things much harder for me. However, I was determined to move on.

He hugged me and said, "It's our baby now, and we'll get through all this stuff together."

He pulled me back into his arms, and we fell fast asleep. Tyrone and I were together two more times before he left.

I was sure that we had the potential to make it work because we wanted to share our life and ministry together. We both went into great detail about what we felt God was calling us to do. We went online to research the cost of church equipment and even checked the prices on rental properties in this area. It all was coming together. I saw everything I had prayed to God about in Tyrone. I wanted someone who loved God, someone who was musically inclined (he played two instruments and sang), someone who was pleasing to the eyes, and someone I was sexually compatible with. Every one of my boxes was checked. However, I still needed to hear from God. I had to have confirmation before I made a commitment of this magnitude to him.

As we stood outside the bus terminal, Tyrone said, "Ann, will you please marry me."

I said, "Let me go home and pray about it now that I have time alone. "

He said, "I understand."

I told him. "I would come visit him next month."

He agreed, and we kissed. He went to get on the bus. I really hated to see him go. I guess I got used to him being here.

As I started praying, God responded quickly with a scripture from Hosea 1. It is the passage where the prophet Hosea marries the prostitute, Gomer. God said, "He is one of mine; he is called and needs to be restored." He went on to say that Tyrone had been broken, and God wanted to use me to heal him. "So yes, you can marry him; there is a purpose." I took a deep breath and made my decision. Then a pastor friend of mine called and said, "God told me to tell you yes, it's ok for you to marry him." I said, "Wow. God has confirmed his Word." I called Tyrone and said, "Yes, I will marry you. God has confirmed His Word to me." He was so happy. He said, "I'm going to start making plans to come down there for good. I would like to be down there within the next two to three weeks." I said, "Alright, sounds good."

Tyrone made it home just in time to go to work that night. However, within the next few days, he was told by his landlord that the property he was living in was being sold. He said he really didn't know what he was going to do because it was in a good location for him to catch the bus to work, and he would also need a short-term lease because he was moving here. He went on to say that having a criminal record was not going to help. I said, "Is it possible for you to move down here earlier than you expected?"

He said, 'No, because it had to be approved by his county, and my county had to accept him. He said, "And it takes time."

I could hear it in his voice that he was concerned.

Tyrone's phone calls became very sporadic. I had no clue as to what was going on with him. So, when he finally contacted me, he said that he was now homeless and sleeping on the streets and that he could only call when he was in a place where he could charge his phone. I noticed that his demeanor was starting to change. He became more irritated and seemed depressed. He started snapping at me over the smallest disagreement.

I finally asked, "Why can't you go stay with your family?" He yelled, "They don't care about me like that. I have no one. Ann, it was my brother who sold the property even though I was paying him rent. I hate to ask, but it's cold out here. Can you send me some money?"

I immediately prayed, and God said, "Send it!" I sent Tyrone $250, which held him in a motel for a while.

His daughter was soon to age out of the Department of Social Services, and he had no place for her to go. All of this was weighing on him, and I was starting to hear it more and more in his voice.

The time for him to come had come and gone, and he had not mentioned what he intended to do, so I decided to make a trip home to see my family and check on him. He asked me to pick him up from work on the way to town. I agreed. Once there, we went back to my daughter's house, where he took a shower and went to bed. While he slept, I washed, dried, and folded clothes, being careful not to wake him. After several hours, I heard him stirring around in the room, so I went in to talk to him. I said, "I washed your uniform, and it's in the dryer." He nodded. Tyrone was very agitated, so I kissed him to encourage him that we would get through this. He said, "All you want to do is have sex."

I said, "No, I want you to know that God will work this out."

He said, "God!" and kind of grunted.

I said, "Can we talk now?"

He nodded.

I said, "What's going on? I thought you were moving down?"

He said, "No!"

I said, "Wait a minute, I need you to explain."

He said, "It's because of you."

I looked at him, feeling very confused because what could I have possibly done other than try to be supportive?

Tyrone said, "You're always talking about Jesus, but God has taken everything from me, and now I am homeless. If you want to support me, stay down here so that I will have a place to stay until I get back on my feet."

I said, "I cannot do that. God placed me where I am to do ministry. You said that you wanted a new start and wanted to come to the beach."

He said, "Listen, that's not going to happen."

I said, "So what you're saying is that you've changed your mind."

He said, "How can I even think about that and have no place to lay my head. I work overtime to keep from being on the streets, and on my days off, I sleep behind buildings in the middle of winter. God has left me."

Tyrone dropped his head and started to cry. "I'm afraid that I'm going to die on these streets. Ann, please stay and help me."

I told him that I would be there for the weekend but had responsibilities at home that I needed to handle. This seemed to disappoint and anger him; however, he continued to weep bitterly.

I asked, "Are you ready to eat?"

"Yes," he said.

I handed him his clothes, and we headed to get burgers and fries. Tyrone ordered two whoppers, two fries, and two drinks. I looked at him like, seriously, dude.

I said, "God, what's going on?"

He said, "Pay it!"

God said, "I want you to take care of him this weekend. You are sowing seeds."

I did as God instructed, but the closer I got to going home, the more belligerent he became, at least in private. When my daughter was around, he pretended to be the perfect fiancé. I grew tired and was ready to go home; however, I still had another day to be there. Tyrone slept in the spare bedroom, and I slept on the chair in the living room. I knew that I would at least get rest during the night because he was constantly begging me to stay longer during the day. However, God never told me to stay, so I stayed with the plan and endured his abuse for not giving in to his demands. I felt bad for him because he had a true need, but he didn't follow God's plan. I honestly didn't know what happened between him coming to see me and him being back home. I didn't understand why he would choose to be on the street versus reaching out to family or coming to be with me at the beach.

I must admit that we found ourselves in the bed once. I think he was trying to persuade me to stay, but after he realized I wasn't going to change my mind.

I remember him grabbing me by the neck, saying, "You're going to do what I say, or I'm going to choke the fuck out of you."

I said, "What?"

He repeated it, and I said, "Get off me now!"

I started to pack, and God said, "No, complete your assignment!"

Tyrone then said, "I'm hungry; take me to get something to eat."

Hesitantly, I said, "Let's go."

I tried to stay quiet even though Tyrone was going off. I couldn't take not one more fuck this, and he didn't give a fuck about me.

I said, "Pastor," trying to remind him of who he was. He continued, so I stopped my car and said, "Get out!" I said, "I have done nothing but try and be supportive of you. I have sent you money to get you off the street and to feed you. I have been taking you to work every day since I have been here, and you are sitting in my car, in which I make the payments, and disrespect me. "Get out!" He said, "This is supposed to be the coldest night of the year, and you are going to put me out?"

I said, "Yes because evidently, you don't mind it being the coldest night of the year. I am not taking any more of your crap. I will be glad when tomorrow comes so I can leave and never hear from you again."

He got out, and I turned around and went back to my daughter's house. After about ten minutes, the phone rang, and he apologized and asked me to come get him.

God said, "Go."

I said, "Where are you? I'm on the way.

When I picked him up, he was frozen to the bone. He was shivering and asked me to cut the heat up. He said, "I am so hungry and would be grateful if you could get me something to eat."

I nodded and stopped at Subway, and returned to my daughter's house. When my daughter came home, I noticed that Tyrone was doing a lot of talking to my daughter. He pretended that everything was fine with us by coming over and placing my feet in his lap.

I said, "Tyrone, not today."

"Ann, please don't do this in front of your daughter," he said. "We will be okay."

In my mind, he was right because he would soon be a memory in the back of my mind. I focused on watching the movie Cara had put on, and the drama of the day faded away. He continued to engage my daughter for the rest of the night. I woke up to a dark room, Tyrone had gone to bed, and my daughter was asleep in her room. I lay there in silence, excited about the drive home the next day. I eventually fell back asleep with a smile on my face.

I was right back up at 7 am. I wanted to get my online church service out the way and then start packing. I wanted to spend a little more time with my mother before heading home. I knew I was going to drop Tyrone off at work on my way home. As soon as the service was over, Tyrone called me to the room because he needed to talk.

I said, "Yes, Tyrone. He said Ann, please don't go. I can't stand thinking about being cold and sleeping on the streets tomorrow night."

I said, "Tyrone, you need to reach out to your family." He said, "Are you doing this because I changed my mind about us getting married?"

I said, "No, actually, I'm ok with it."

He said, "You never loved me. You loved him."

I said, "You're right, but you knew that before things got to this point." He said, "Ann, please!"

I said, "Once and for all, no, I'm headed home today."

I heard Tyrone ask my daughter to accept his Facebook request. She said she would. I paid her for letting us stay, kissed her, and headed to my mom's house. Tyrone was the perfect gentleman the entire time we were at my mom's house.

However, when I started down the road to his job, he looked at me and said, "You know your daughter is cooler to be around than you?"

I nodded because I was waiting for this. I knew he had been giving my daughter a lot of attention for a reason.

Tyrone said, "You know she accepted my friend request?"

I said, 'That's good."

"Tyrone, look, if my mother or daughter knew about how you were treating me, trust me, they would not give you the time of day. But don't ever think you will come between me and my daughter. That will never happen."

He became belligerent, saying, "I don't give a fuck about you or your daughter. How dare you? I would never mess with your daughter."

"Like I said to you before, you can calm down or get out. Your choice. God has instructed me to get you dinner and drop you off at work; it's up to you whether I complete this assignment."

He quieted down because he knew I had had enough and would put him out on the street and he would have to get to work the best way he could. I did just as God instructed. I bought an 8-piece box of chicken for him. He took five pieces and left me three. When I pulled into his job, he didn't say a word; he just got out, slammed the door, and walked inside the building.

As I started driving away, the Lord told me to call Cara and inform her of what He had shown me. I told her that Tyrone was going to contact her because he needed a place to stay. I said, "His intention is to hurt me, but Tyrone is not allowed to come back to your house without me being there for any reason."

She said, "Mama, he's already in boxed me on Facebook messenger, asking if he can talk to me. I'm going to block him."

I said, "If he ever shows up there, call the police because he is a convicted rapist."

"Should I be afraid?" she asked

"No, because I will tell him what you are going to do."

She said, "Okay."

I didn't hear from Tyrone for about two days; however, he was back to his disrespectful self. I hung up. He called back a week later, saying, "I'm sorry for everything, but I was not interested in your daughter that way."

I said, "I understand, but what do you want. It was my plan never to hear from you again."

He said, "Ann, I need some help. I said are you really calling me to help you after the way you behaved?"

He said, "I am because I have no one else to ask."

I said, "Tyrone, what's going on?"

"My daughter is getting ready to age out of DSS, and I must get a place for her to stay so she can come live with me," he said.

I said, "What do you need me to do?"

He said, "I need money."

I took a deep breath and said, "I'll pray about it."

He said, "Okay, please get back to me soon. I'm working overtime but need some help."

When I prayed about it, and God told me to help him, I was floored. I ended up sending Tyrone about two thousand dollars over the course of three months. His attitude changed, and we started to become friends. We talked every day but understood that was as far as our relationship would go. He was able to find a place and furnish it. He then said, "Ann, I need some more help."

I said, "What now?"

He said, “It’s furnished, but I don’t have any towels, washcloths, or sheets.” I went into my closet and filled up a garbage bag full of those items.

He then said, “I have been approved, but I need you to take me to pick her up.”

I said, “Where is she?”

He said, “In a group home not too far from you. Please let me catch the bus to you, and you can take me to get my baby the next morning and then drive us back to Columbia.”

I said, “Tyrone, listen, I don’t have a problem with helping you because that is what my outreach is about, but I’m not sure about you coming back here to the house.”

He said, “Ann, none of that is on my mind. I only want to bring my daughter home!”

I said, “You promise.

He said, “Yes, I know where your heart is, and it's not with me.”

I said, “Then, set it up, and I will do it.”

Tyrone seemed sincere about making his daughter a priority. He said he didn’t have room for anything else. He started asking me questions about how to raise a daughter.

I said, “She will be eighteen years old and full of herself. All girls go through this phase, but you are going to have to set rules for your house. Know that she is going to play the ‘You weren’t there for me card.’ Be loving and supportive, but be her dad and not her friend. There must be a line drawn where she understands that you are the parent, and she must follow your rules. Don't forget to give her responsibilities around the house, but let her know that she has a choice of going to school or getting a job. This will limit her time alone at home, which will keep the boys away."

He said, "Wow. I have a lot to learn."

I said, "You'll get it!"

He said, "That's why I need you in my life."

I said, "Please don't start." He said, "I don't mean it like that, just as someone I can talk to."

I said, "God will send you someone that you can trust and depend on for this type of thing."

He said, "I'm not sure if that's what I want. I just need to be a dad for right now."

I said, "Tyrone, I suggest strongly that you rebuild your relationship with God because both of you are going to need Him. There is a lot of healing that needs to happen with you and your daughter. You can only be her dad, not her God. I am sure that she has gone through a lot in those nine years. She's going to need time to process it all. Find her a counselor, but most importantly, find a church that she can attend."

He said he understood.

Tyrone called a few days before coming down to ensure I was still going to help. I told him everything was a go. He gave me the dates and times and sent pictures of his new home. He was proud because he was no longer on the streets, and he had made his new apartment a home. He felt as though his life was starting to look up.

He only needed to get his daughter home to complete his dream of having his baby home with him.

Tyrone arrived here on time that Friday before his daughter was to be released. He was noticeably happy but nervous as well. He wanted everything to be perfect, so he asked if I knew a place where he could get his haircut. I made the appointment and texted the barber that I would be sowing a seed by paying for his haircut. I told him to do whatever he wanted. The barber was the director of music at my church. Therefore, he knew my heart was to help whomever I could. I took Tyrone to get something to eat and then dropped him off at the barbershop. I told him to call me when he was ready. About an hour and a half later, I sent payment and went to pick him up. He looked like a brand-new person. His confidence was up, and he said, "Thank you, Ann, the barber told me what you did. I'm grateful!"

He said, "I was so busy trying to get the house ready and planning her birthday party that I completely forgot about a haircut."

I said, "It's cool!"

I texted the barber to see if I had sent enough, and he said it was fine because after hearing his story, he also wanted to be a blessing to him.

Tyrone was ready. We went to get something to eat and then settled in for the night. I had gone to bed, and Tyrone was on the chair watching television, I believe. However, I heard him moving around. I called out to him, saying, "Are you alright?"

He said, "Yes, but I can't rest because I'm going to see my baby tomorrow. I'm extremely nervous because I don't know how I am going to react to seeing her. I may break down and cry."

I said, 'That will be fine too."

He said, "Ann, I could not have done this without you."

I said, "Thank God because he was the one who told me to do it."

He said, "You are a good woman."

I checked the time and realized that it was time to pray.

I started praying three times a day as God had instructed for Terrell. I didn't know why, but I'd just learned to be obedient. Tyrone left the room to give me privacy, and I began to pray the Word of God over Terrell's life. Now, I felt Tyrone come into the room; in fact, he stood directly in front of me. However, I didn't stop praying. He turned around and walked back out of the room.

After I finished, Tyrone came back, and we continued to talk about his daughter. I started getting sleepy and wanted to turn it in because we had an early morning. She needed to be picked up by 9 am, and she was almost forty-five minutes away. So, I laid down fully dressed to make sure there was no misunderstandings. Tyrone kneeled over the top of me and started to rip my clothes off. I said, "No, we're not doing this!"

He didn't respond. He became aggressive the more I fought him. I felt powerless that something like this was happening, especially after everything I had done for him.

I prayed, saying, "God, search my heart now, please!" When he finally spoke, he said, "So, you don't want it."

I said, "Tyrone, I don't live like this anymore. I reconsecrated my body back to God, and you're violating me. Tyrone, this one is on you."

Just as he reached his climax, he said, "I'm going to show you this nigga ain't got nothing on me."

The tears rolled down my face, and I was mad as hell because he promised that all he wanted to do was get his child home.

Afterward, he had the nerve to lie down beside me and go to sleep. I got up and went to my office and continued to cry. I began to doubt whether I had been hearing God's voice. I couldn't understand why God would allow me to go through this. I had already been through molestation, rape, and now this! I thought about killing him, but the truth is I knew who he was before this happened. I let him come because God told me to, or at least I thought He told me to. Honestly, right now, I just didn't know. I could hear the enemy say, "But this is the God you serve?. He is the reason this happened."

I began to pray, "God, why?"

"Ann, I need you to finish your assignment."

"I can't God."

"You can!"

"I promise you that Tyrone won't get away with anything. However, I will deal with him, not the prison system, and his daughter is a key part of it."

I got on the phone and called a close sister in Christ, Pat, who agreed to ride with me to take them back to Columbia.

Tyrone realized that I was no longer in the bed, so he started searching for me throughout the house.

When he entered my office, he said, "Ann, what's wrong?"

"Tyrone, you promised. We have come so far; why would you do this?"

"So, you really didn't want it."

"Tyrone, why don't you understand I don't live like that anymore. This one is on you. God is going to deal with you for what you've done tonight. You violently violated me. I hurt all over all because you heard me praying for Terrell. I'm not with Terrell. I was given an assignment to pray for him just as I was given an assignment to help you. I will complete that assignment tomorrow, and I never want to hear from you again."

Tyrone turned and walked out the door as if he had done nothing. I later found him in my bed asleep. I laid down and cried myself to sleep that night.

I woke up early the next morning and started cleaning the kitchen. Tyrone came and stood beside me. I think he was hoping that I felt differently, but the pain in my body was a reminder of what he did to me.

He said, "Good morning."

I turned and stared him straight in the eyes, not saying a word.

"He said, "Ann!"

"Get away from me, I yelled!"

He slowly walked away and started to get dressed. It took about forty minutes for us to get dressed and pack the car. Before I knew it, we were on our way. It was a long, quiet ride to pick his daughter up.

Once there, I backed in and remained in the car. He invited me to go in with him to sign the papers and to finally meet his daughter.

I didn't respond.

So, he proceeded to handle his business. After about twenty minutes, he started to load his daughter's belongings in the car. Once he was done, he brought his daughter out and introduced her to me. I spoke, and we were on our way to pick up Pat.

He then whispered, "I don't think we will have room for your friend to go."

I said, "Then, I guess some of your daughters' things won't be going."

Once I got to Pat's house, her husband rearranged the car so that Pat could go and all his daughter's belongings as well. The four of us were on our way, and Pat asked if she could drive.

I said, "Yes, because she drives fast."

I figured that's less time I had to spend with him. Pat talked to his daughter and thought it was strange that I wasn't saying anything. She asked if I was alright? I nodded my head because I didn't want to involve the daughter. I asked Pat to stop so that we could get gas. I got out, paid, and started pumping. Tyrone went inside to get some snacks for him and his daughter. When he returned to the car, he grabbed the handle of the gas pump and said, "I will pump."

I said, "Please, get away from me. I have it."

He said, "I will not sit in the car while women pump the gas."

I said, "Oh, you're worried about what people will say about you. Why didn't that matter last night?"

He said, "Ann, please go get in the car; I've got it."

I walked away, getting in the car. As we traveled, I talked with Pat in the front, and he talked with his daughter in the back seat. Before long, we were pulling into their driveway.

Tyrone, Pat, and I started to unload the car while his daughter went to check out her new home. Once everything was out, Tyrone asked if I wanted to come in and see the place.

He said, "Ann, without you, it wouldn't be possible."

I said, "No, I'm not coming in. Our business is now completed. Please, do not call me again."

Pat and I got in the car and headed home. However, we didn't get far before

Pat asked, "What happened?" I explained what he did and how my body was still in pain from what he did. She was furious!

She said, "I knew that man was no good. I'm glad that he is out of your life now. He never sat right with me. I know I didn't know him, but I just felt he wasn't the right man for you." She said, "Wait on Terrell; God will do it!"

I said, "I'm not interested in anyone right now. I just need time to get it together."

"I promise you will get through this," she said.

I said, "I honestly don't know who I am madder at, him, me or God."

She said, "God?"

I said, "Yes, because I prayed about this man before I ever met him, and God said yes. I don't understand how all of this happened. For the first time, I prayed, and it still didn't work."Our conversation gave way to the oldies music that was playing,

Once I got home, I broke down and cried uncontrollably for days. I was overcome with the feeling and need to know why. I felt anger rising in me; however, who was I angry with?

I said, "God, please tell me why this had to happen."

He said, "Because you are faithful and prayed to me about it."

I said, "I didn't pray to be hurt in this way."

He said, "No, but you prayed for me to send another. I told you that Terrell would protect you from those who would harm you while you're serving through outreach. I needed to show you what was out there. But know that Tyrone won't get away with it. I need you to forgive Tyrone and trust me concerning Terrell."

I said, "How, Lord? I'm hurt. "

He said, "By depending on me."

I spent another four weeks praying, studying, and fasting. I also spent a lot of time crying out to God because I wasn't going to let the devil win, not again. It was the only way I was going to survive this because I felt my mind slipping. However, I praised and worshipped my way through, and God was faithful. I learned a valuable lesson from this. When you are obedient, be careful of the prayers you pray because you just may get what you prayed for.

I know now that it is imperative to trust and obey God without faltering. This is how the Proverbs 31 woman accomplishes all that she does. She puts God first! I, too, must keep God first in order to be all God intends. The scripture concerning this woman makes her appear perfect. However, the Word of God says no one is; it states we all fall short of the glory of God. If this is true, I believe this scripture is a guide on how to become a better woman and/or wife. Therefore, I've decided to make a conscious decision to keep God first by following His will and His way. I will attain some resemblance of her by allowing His love to continually transform me from the inside out!

I intentionally focused on God because what the enemy meant for my bad God had turned around for my good. I was stronger and now wiser. I now understand that the quality of my life was rooted and grounded in Jesus. So, I now embrace the will of God in my life.

Now, with that being said, God instructed me to go back to leadership in my church. Nothing seemed to change there, but I had, and it has made all the difference in the world. God told me to make sure I only speak the Word and let them wrestle with His truth. I followed that regardless of what is being said or done.

Many don't understand and even reject the word because it's coming from me. It no longer bothers me because it's their life.

I am so happy and full of joy and peace, all because of God. I remember one day while praying, the Lord spoke to me these words:

"Ann, you've read the story about the narrow road and the wide road. I want you to become comfortable being alone. You may be physically alone, but you will never be lonely because I am with you. People are going to hate you because you speak my truth. Everything you have and are is because of me, and you freely acknowledge it. That will expose others who don't have the same heart. You are on the right road where few travel. Beware of crowds; they represent the wide road and conform to the world's standards. Stand even when you don't understand."

"Yes, Lord," I said.

These Words have guided my life in ministry and family since I heard them. However, Terrell was another story. I needed peace concerning him, and God did just that. I had to accept where he was in his walk. As I said early on, Terrell and I were a lot alike, but we all have to come to God for ourselves. It took me many years to find the peace I desperately needed. He was no different.

I got out of my feelings and gave him to Jesus. I prayed a simple prayer. God, you did it for me. I know that you can and will do it for him. It is your will that we become one. I trust and believe that in your time, all will be revealed. Amen

God put me to the test quickly. I allowed one of the ministers to use my vehicle for thirty days. On the day I was to get back, I had taken the spare key to a friend so she could drive it home from the church. My friend got tied up at her church, and I had no one to get it home. Terrell walked out of the church, and the Spirit said ask him to drive the truck home while you drive the car. Long story short, he agreed!

Now, what he didn't know was that he was driving the truck that God told me to get for him. It was supposed to be a wedding gift, and he had no clue. He was standing outside a house that he was supposed to partly own. I heard the Lord say, "I'm speaking to him now!"

I quickly changed my shoes and got back into the car to take him back to get his vehicle. As we headed back, my phone rang, and it was Pat asking if I had gotten the car home. I told her Terrell had driven it, and I was now headed back to take him to get his car. I asked her to fix me a plate for dinner, and she said, "Fix your own plate," and then asked Terrell if he wanted something to eat. He said, "No," which shocked me because normally, he wouldn't want anyone to know, but he was actually having a conversation with Pat and her husband. It felt so normal. I said be there soon and hung up. As I pulled into the church parking lot, I thanked him and drove away.

About three days before Father's Day, I heard the Lord say, "I want you to do something for Terrell in appreciation of him helping you and because it is Father's Day." I said, "Lord, what should I do?" He said, "You have a friend that sells cologne; call her." I did, and she said she had something that she thought he might like. I asked the price and headed her way that night to pick it up.

On my way there, a storm came up suddenly, and I was stuck in it. I couldn't believe it because the skies were clear when I left home. Now, the skies were dark, lightning was flashing, and rain was falling. I could barely see to get back home. However, I slowed down and took my time. People were driving recklessly, but after about forty-five minutes, I pulled back into my yard and ran inside just as I heard another lightning strike.

I sat down and wondered why God wanted me to do this. I told him thank you before he got out of the car. God didn't speak. I prepared for bed because I had some running around to do the next morning. With this virus going on, I try to move around early before people start moving around.

The next morning, I got up at 7 am and was out the door by 7:30. I was able to get my sister's birthday card, and I also looked for a card for Terrell to go with the cologne. I found one for each, both sweet, simple, and to the point. I paid and started home, trying to determine what I was going to put on his card. We weren't really friends at this point; in fact he was just someone I saw in church. There was no personal conversation between us, not even a good morning or goodbye. However, he watched me all the time as service went on. What could I say, or do I let the card speak for me? God still didn't speak!

I got home and sat at my desk, waiting for God to speak. I started to write, realizing that I was writing a card for my sister on the card that I had bought for Terrell. I said, "Holy Spirit, why didn't you warn me?" God said, "I don't want you to give him a card. I want you to do a letter speaking from your heart. I finished my sister's card and sat before my computer, praying and asking the Lord to speak through me. This is what God gave me.

Dear Terrell,

I know this may come as a surprise to you, but God has placed something on my heart concerning you. I went to the store, like most people, to find the perfect card. I thought I had until I got back home, and God said the truth is I wanted to keep it light, but God had a different plan. So here goes. You are an amazing man despite all that you have gone through in your life. Your heart is big. Although you have tried to hide it, I have seen it many times.

I want you to know that I love you and probably always will. I got tired of choosing between the love I have for God and the love I have for you. Why should I have to choose? I wanted to be with you forever, but I will settle for a friend every now and again as you permit because I respect your right to feel as you do. You cannot make someone love you. However, I freely chose to love you, and I will never be sorry for that. Though my life seems less bright without you in it, I am learning to make the necessary adjustments to get through the day. It is funny because your presence is still in and around the house. In fact, it was weird seeing you stand outside a house that you were supposed to partly own or drive a truck that should have been a gift to you. Everything that has been done here has been to what I thought you would like, and now you're gone. That is how much I believed in you and me. I put it all on the line and came up short, but I have no regrets. I have prayed and asked God to remove me from the church and to remove you from my heart just to give each of us a chance to move on, but here I am still at the church and loving you.

My prayer for you is that one day, you will allow someone to truly love you. Someone who will put you first. Someone who will love you and not what they think you possess. Someone who loves your successes but also loves you through your failures. Someone who will listen and someone who knows when to pray. Someone who loves God first so that they can love you the way you need to be loved. Let's face it, you cannot spend your entire life in the bed. Lol. This was and is how I have loved you all these years. I believe, with everything in me, that we were each other's second chance. I pray God grants you another one because you so deserve it!

In closing, I know you do not see it, and to be honest, it's ok because I did not write this to sway you. I wrote it because it is the truth. You are a mighty man of God, and He will use you to bring others to Him. You will stand in a pulpit or platform decreeing God's Word, and people will come. Terrell, you have no idea of how these five years have affected me. When it was good, it was very good, and when it was bad, it got very bad, but my love for you survived it all. It really has worked out for my good. I pray one day, you, too, will experience the love, peace, and goodness that I have come to enjoy daily. I love you enough to be honest about how I feel about you, excepting that you do not feel the same and being fine with that. I pray that we can eventually be friends because I really miss hearing your take on the Word, politics, and everything else. Never forget that someone loves you and that someone always will. God bless.

PS. Thank you for helping me out Sunday, and Happy Father's Day.

Sincerely, Ann

I presented it to him in an envelope with the cologne and a special gift that will remain anonymous. I called and asked him to meet me because I didn't want to give it to him at church. He agreed. We met in a strip mall not far from my house the next day.

He was surprised and said, "Ann, you didn't have to do this," repeatedly as he went through the bag. He opened the cologne and said, "Oh, I like this. It smells like one that I have at home."

He leaned in to let me smell it. Oh, my goodness, I could've fainted right there. He smelled so good.

"What about this mystery gift?" He asked.

I said, "Surely you recognized it because you were the one who told me to get it."

He laughed and said, "You hold it!"

When he got to the letter, I said, "No, read it once you get home."

He thanked me, and we each went in separate directions. God had answered my prayers because I didn't know if I had it in me to be that close to him. After all, I was and am still in love with him. I went home and imagined as girls do when their prince charming finally comes. Though we are not as close as we used to be, we talk from time to time. As I said in the letter, I am content with being his friend every now and again. However, I know that God is not finished with us yet.

Looking back, I see several things you should get out of this chapter. First, God speaking to you about a situation is not a license to sin against Him. Sometimes, He will reveal things as a warning, and other times, He allows things to happen because of human nature to bring you to that place in Him. What do I mean? God had chosen Terrell for me as a husband, but I flat-out refused and asked for another. So, God sent Tyrone. God had to show me how bad things could get for me to appreciate what He was already offering me. What I went through with Tyrone was so much worse than what I went through with Terrell. However, Tyrone was the relationship that sealed my fate when it came to my faith. I've learned to trust and depend on God regardless of what a situation looks like. This was not on God but on me, all because of my disobedience.

You have to understand that God has been talking to me throughout my life. The problem was I simply didn't understand or just wanted to do what I wanted to do. He was building my faith and teaching me to trust Him and not what I saw or felt. Terrell hurt me; therefore, I wanted to get as far away from him as I could. The problem was that I may have changed my mind, but God didn't change His. There was more than a relationship at stake. God was building ministry and purpose through what was supposed to be our union. I just didn't have the heart to believe in it anymore. In essence, I lost my faith in God to fix it.

Have you ever lost your faith that God could change your situation?

Has God ever asked you to do something, and you refused, causing terrible consequences?

Secondly, there were times that I felt I should have left or ended my help to Tyrone, but God said, "No, complete your assignment." The only way I can explain this is obedience. Disobedience got me into the situation, and I knew I had to finish what God was calling me to do. I know that I am being called to be a Pastor. When God assigns you to a certain ministry or people, you can't walk away just because things get tough. You're fighting for the soul of the person. This chapter is about God training me. He was training me to hear his voice and to trust His ways. I can honestly say I had a hard time accepting some of the things God said, but I can say that as horrible as it was, I made it to where God wanted me to get. So, are you willing to listen to the voice of God even when it goes against everything you or other people believe, trusting that you will come out of your situation better? Know that God will move according to His Spirit and not how we feel about a situation. Everything I did for Tyrone became a seed that launched my outreach in the area of helping the homeless and those needing food. I had a firsthand look at what it took to help sustain someone. There is not one area of my life that I cannot help someone in. You can't help in an area you yourself have no knowledge of. You will throw money or resources at it and not understand what caused the deficit. That is where the help is needed the most because, like me, you will continue in the cycle until you learn to do something different. My difference was God. His way is different from the world's way. Being molested drew me to a molester. Being raped drew a rapist to me, and so on and so on, not to judge but to help. Every person throughout this journey—me included—needed healing and deliverance.

God sacrificed Jesus for the world. Instead of judging us, He redeemed us. We, too, must lay down our lives and all we think we know for the winning of souls. We will go through many things, but with God, we shall emerge victorious prayerfully with another soul won for the kingdom of God. I am not perfect, and neither are you; however, we serve a perfect God who will use not some of our lives but all to bring us to His expected end. God loves us, and He showed it through His sacrifice.

Know that Tyrone raped me, but God dealt with him. He called sometime later to say he was wrong and that he ended up in the hospital, almost dying. He said that he was now ready to walk in what God was calling him to do and be. We are now friends, and we talk every now and again.

God has a plan and purpose for all our lives. What are you willing to sacrifice for it today?

I've decided to do this thing God's way regardless of what I had to go through. God, I will wait on you concerning Terrell. Like Ruth, I will glean in the field until he shows up.

CHAPTER NINE

The 9th Hour: It is Finished!

We have finally reached the end of this journey. However, I wanted to leave you with revelations that could change your life forever if you choose to apply them. I need to add a disclaimer here. I am a believer, and therefore, everything I have shared with you is based on that fact. You see, nothing else worked for me, and in essence, I was pleading with God to take me to heaven immediately if that was going to be my only reward later. I never understood how Jesus dying on the cross would help me live a better life while I was here on earth. The truth is I found nothing but heartache and despair, and the little peeks of happiness that showed up were not enough to sustain me. There had to be more than what I was seeing or even experiencing. I was willing to leave my mother, daughter, friends, and everything else to find peace, but God intervened. I believed the lies of the enemy, and it cost me dearly. You see, looking back now, I realize that I only had a form of godliness but denied the power of God. What do I mean by that? I had been in church most of my life and heard stories about the Man, but most of the people I knew were struggling just as I was. Most of the stories I heard were about eternal life, and I'm not saying that wasn't important, but I needed help now. I wasn't looking for a spiritual ATM to hand me money when I needed it. No, I needed a God that would sustain me despite the season I was in. I needed stability. I needed a father and a confidant. I needed someone that I could always depend on, someone that wouldn't change. I needed someone that loved me unconditionally. The only problem was I had it all the time; I just didn't know it. Instead, I looked for it in the face of man (humanity). This process has taught me that God, through Jesus Christ, was and is enough.

So, when I say it is finished, I mean that I no longer believe the lies of the devil and have embraced all that Jesus is to me. I know I no longer need to look to others to try and figure out what a relationship with God looks like. I reject the abusive relationship that I have had with the devil, and I embrace the love of God because He sent His son to die a brutal death just for me. Who wouldn't serve a God like that.

I want you to see the scripture so that you can get a greater understanding of what Jesus did and how it applies to us.

John 19:30 (NKJ) states, 30 So when Jesus had received the sour wine, He said, "It is finished!" And bowing His head, He gave up His spirit.

Believe it or not, this small passage explains it all. I believe the sour wine represents all the bitterness of life, and Jesus bowing his head and giving up the Spirit is a representation of us dying to self. If we could learn to die to self, the enemy has no way in. We would be completely dependent on God for everything we want and need. You see, the devil attacks us through our desires. He wants to be our God; therefore, he will offer us many things, but they will always come at a price. His goal is to make us think that God is denying us, and, in most cases, we believe it because God isn't moving fast enough for us. I ask you to consider this, God is our creator, and who knows better what we, the creation, need than the one who created us. Honestly, what can the devil offer that God does not already own? I've learned through this journey that it doesn't matter what he offers because it will never be as good as what God has for us. This is found in Matthew 7:11 (KJV),

If ye then, being evil, know how to give good gifts. Unto your children, how much more shall your Father, which is in heaven, give good things to those who ask him!

If you are an unbeliever or believer struggling to make it another day, this book is for you. Here are the steps God walked me through so that I can now walk in freedom.

True Salvation: (Romans 10:9-10) "That if you confess with your mouth, "Jesus is Lord," And believe in your heart that God raised him from the dead, you will be saved. 10 For it is with your heart that you believe and are justified, and it is with your mouth that you confess and are saved." For me, this was my first step because I thought I was living a saved life. However, repentance can only be found when you truly turn away from willful sin, never to do it again. It was the thing that caused the fall back in the Garden of Eden, and it causes men to fall today. The Bible says that we all fall short of God's glory, meaning it's our nature to sin, but we must take a stand against willful sinning. We should never make a conscious decision to sin against God. Think about it, isn't that what Satan did? Understand the Bible says we sin daily; however, we must repent (meaning to turn away from it) and try our best to do better.

Lordship: (1 Corinthians 8:6) Yet for us there is but one God, the Father, from whom are all things, and we exist for Him; and one Lord, Jesus Christ, by whom are all things, and we exist through Him. To make God Lord through Jesus simply means to give Him complete control over your life. It means that He accepts total responsibility for everything concerning you. What I love about this is now I can say, "God, this has to work out because I did what you told me to. I followed your will, and I followed your way, and this doesn't look like what you said." God is obligated to fix it. My job at this point is to wait in God until it turns in my favor. Now, I didn't say wait on God; I said wait in God. There is a difference. When I wait in God, I continue to praise, worship, study, fast, and serve, knowing that God's got this. When I wait on God, I'm not doing anything except watching the clock.

Trust God: (Proverbs 3:5-6) Trust in the LORD with all thine heart; and lean not unto thine own understanding. In all thy ways acknowledge him, and he shall direct thy paths. This was a hard one for me once because just about every person in my life had let me down at some point. So how was I supposed to trust someone I hadn't physically seen? Easy by just looking back. I can hear you saying, "What do you mean?" God had proven Himself to me over and over again. The truth is He has a proven track record with me. I'm sure you, too, have seen the hands of God in your life but, at the time, didn't know it. We sometimes dismiss a move of God and call it luck. If you were like me, I expected the ground to shake and the thunder to roar, you know, something dramatic. However, I've learned that God can move in a small voice that compels someone to act, which may put food in your stomach, a roof over your head, or a change of lane, which may prevent an accident. God can move in any way He chooses. The key is to simply be open to what He wants to do concerning you and leave the how up to Him. I have learned to trust God even when I have no clue as to what He is doing because the truth is I may not know what He's doing, but I know He is doing something, and that gives me peace.

True Deliverance: Galatians 5:1 It is for freedom that Christ has set us free. Stand firm, then, and do not let yourselves be burdened again by a yoke of slavery. Deliverance is not a one-time thing. It is a process that every believer goes through as long as there is breath in our bodies. However, the thing to remember is not to return to those things that God has set you free from. Satan devices are not new; however, they do seem to come in different wrappings. Remember, temptations come from within. Therefore. it is imperative that you submerge yourself in the things of God because only He can change you from the inside out. That way, when the devil comes, he won't find anything to tempt.

Spend Time with the Lord: (Matthew 6:33) But seek first the kingdom of God and his righteousness, and all these things will be added to you. This means before you venture out on your day, spend time with God, learning His ways. This can be done by reading the Word, praying, fasting, or praising and worshipping. Don't forget to allow God to speak to you in those moments. Often, we spout out a list of things we want, and we quickly jump up to be about our day. However, I encourage you to wait for His presence to show up. It is in those moments that change occurs.

I want to share a lesson I learned concerning this concept. I was serving at a smaller ministry a few years ago. My pastor knew my heart was to help in any area I could, so he would rely on me heavily to get certain things done concerning the ministry. Every day, I was up and out of the door to the next project he had me working on. On this one particular morning, I heard the Lord say, "You have made serving your God." I said, "Lord, I don't understand."

He said, "Every day, you run out of this house and bypass me. I don't get a thank you or anything, and it is me who has given you the strength and wisdom to accomplish these things."

I said, "Lord, I thought I was serving you by doing all these things."

He said, "No, you are serving man. From this day forward, you will come to me early, and I will instruct you on what to do on this day."

I said, "Yes, Lord."

I repented at that moment. Understand that good work is not always God's work; always spend time with God first and He will direct your day.

Study the Word: 2 Timothy 2:15 15 Study to shew thyself approved unto God, a workman that need not to be ashamed, rightly dividing the word of truth. It is important to study the Word of God because only then can we learn the heart and mind of God. The Word washes you from all unrighteous (sin). The key to studying the Word is understanding that you will start off reading the scripture, but eventually, it will start reading you. What do I mean? You will begin to see yourself in the Word. However, keep reading because, eventually, you will start to look like Jesus. The Word transforms us into the image of God.

Stand on the Word: 2 Timothy 3:16-17 All Scripture is breathed out by God and profitable for teaching, for reproof, for correction, and for training in righteousness, that the man of God may be competent, equipped for every good work. It is important to stand on every Word of God. It is your road map to being successful in this life, and it is the door to eternal life. Never depart from it. It is your lifeline to all that God has in store for you.

Listen to the voice of God: (Matthew 4:4) Jesus answered, "It is written: 'Man shall not live on bread alone, but on every word that comes from the mouth of God." This is important! People will tell you that God doesn't speak to us today. They will say He only speaks through His Word. Don't believe any of it. Every relationship with God is unique; therefore, just because God doesn't speak to them doesn't mean He is not talking to you. I was mocked and literally talked about because of things God told me. People don't like it when you have a mind of your own, and they don't like it when God takes you in a direction different from the norm. However, I encourage you to stand firm on what you know and believe. How will I know the voice of God, you say? It is simple. God will never ask you to go against His will, His character, or His Word. The only way you will know His will or character is to learn His Word. I'm going to warn you, most of the things God has spoken to me isolated me from the pack. People weren't pleased, but God was, and that's all that mattered to me.

Bad Things Happen: (Matthew 5:45) That ye may be the children of your Father which is in heaven: for He makes His sun to rise on the evil and on the good and sends rain on the just and on the unjust. I remember asking God why bad things happen to good people. This scripture was His response. We may not be doing things the way the world does them; however, we physically live in this world, and things happen. However, the most important thing to remember is that God will be with you in it, and He will see you through it. We call these times a test of our faith. Without trials and tribulations, we would never know how good God is to us. At some point in our lives, He has been Savior, deliverer, healer, provider, and protector, just to name a few He has been to me.

The storms that I spoke about in this book were representations of the storms I was facing in my life. The worse my life got, the worse the rain/storms got. As my life got better, the storms did, too. One was a natural storm, but the other was spiritual. We all go through these seasons, but know you will never go through them alone. God will always be there!

Manifested Promises: (2 Corinthians 1:20) For no matter how many promises God has made, they are "Yes" in Christ. And so, through him, the "Amen is spoken by us to the glory of God. Everything God promised will happen in due time and due season. I am a living witness to this truth. I am now walking in promises He made over twenty years ago. I want you to understand I am not bragging on me but God because without Him, I wouldn't be here today to encourage you.

God has given me a better understanding of who He is to me, and I found that it is not based on the opinions of others. I found out that He really loves me and desires the best for me. Through my process, He took away every hurt and pain I had and replaced it with joy and gratefulness. I realized that the people I have encountered in my life were like me in their process. Unfortunately, that doesn't always look good. In fact, it can be messy and downright ugly. However, I choose not to follow the path of the devil but to give them grace and mercy just as God had given me. I choose not to judge but to love just as God loves me. This breaks the back of the devil and frees me to be all that God purposed. I no longer believe the lie that has been instilled in me since childhood. I do matter, and God can use me. The enemy started early in my life, so I would not recognize who or what I was called to do. He buried me under the weight of my failures and shame, but I have learned to cast my cares on the Lord by embracing the sacrifice of Jesus on the cross and all it represents. The voice of God has become louder than the voice of Satan, which renders Him powerless.

I am grateful for eternal life, but I also am now thankful to God for this life and all of its twists and turns. The truth is I wouldn't be the woman I am today without them. God used all my life (not just the good) to bring me to this expected end, and I will serve Him for the rest of my life.

God has Healed Me: This is another area that I am pleased about. Years ago, I was sexually assaulted, and I remember the devil telling me to gain weight and then I would become invisible to men and be safe. I believed him and went from 129 pounds to 350 in thirty years. Now, it was not my intention to gain all of this weight, but once it started, I lost control. The depression of what happened to me fueled my eating, and before you know it, I had all kinds of health issues. I also suffered from anxiety, panic attacks, and suicidal thoughts. I started taking all kinds of medications. They range from anti-depression, diabetes, high blood pressure, high cholesterol, and pills for knee pain, just to name a few. My nightstand had no room for anything else because of the bottles of pills that sat there.

I decided I wasn't going to live like that any longer. I prayed and asked God for guidance. He instructed me to have bariatric surgery. I went to my doctor to ask if he felt I was a good candidate for it. He agreed. I researched and immediately started a program in my hometown. I completed the program and had surgery on November 23, 2021. I guess God was testing me with the date, seeing as Thanksgiving was two days away. However, I did well. I wasn't tempted by any of the food my family was eating. It has been almost two years, and I am off all my meds but 1, and my doctor said I am doing well. Though I have a long way to go, I am excited for the journey because the devil had his plan, but God intervened again. Today, I am 200 pounds down and feeling wonderful.

I was also diagnosed with a blood clot, an ulcer, and a mass in my upper right thigh, which was the size of a small grapefruit; it came back clear of no cancer. My OBGYN also found a lump in my right breast eight months ago, and two months ago, they couldn't find any signs of it. I'd broken my right foot and broken my toe on the left foot. Why am I mentioning all of this? Because God had a plan, and the devil tried to stop that plan with sickness, disease, and death, but God. What I need you to understand is the closer I got to my deliverance, the more aggressive the enemy became. I need you to recognize the devices of Satan. His goal is to control the mind, so the initial sexual assault as a child started a snowball, which became my life. So, God healed me spiritually, and then healing took place in me physically. I thank Him for giving me a second chance.

I am 6 classes from completing my bachelor's degree in Christian Ministry and am licensed and ordained in two denominations (Baptist and Non-denominational). The goal is to one day pastor a ministry that will be sold out to God. I mean one that will help the poor, care for the homeless, feed the hungry, and clothe the naked. This ministry will go after the unsaved and train the believer all in the name of God. We are going back to the original assignment of the church.

God Has Blessed Me: I became very active in helping others during the pandemic. I didn't go out and stockpile supplies. In truth, I only kept enough for myself. However, everything in the world was uncertain, and people were suffering more than usual. I wanted and needed to be a blessing in any way I could. In truth, I didn't have much, but God has a way of taking little and making it much. I prayed a simple prayer, and He said, "Use what you have." So, I started using extra cash, loans, and credit cards to help people that God had placed in my path. Once the season of sowing was over, I prayed, "God, I have done as you said. Please help me pay off all these bills."

God said again, "Use what you have."

I didn't understand; however, God spoke and said, "Use your house."

You know, we sometimes look for God to do supernatural things when He has already given us everything we need to sustain us. I made a few phone calls and decided to refinance my house. I was able to pay almost all my bills except for those that dealt with the house and car insurance. I got a lower interest rate, and it saved me over fifteen hundred dollars a month. God also took a hundred-thousand-dollar student loan and reduced it to thirty-nine dollars a month for three years, which will total fifteen hundred dollars when I make the last payment.

God Healed my Relationship with my Family: I am so blessed to be a part of such an awesome family. I've learned to accept people as they are regardless of who they are; my family is no different. Over the years, I have learned a lot about our family history, and I now understand why we are the way we are. I'm grateful for each one of them because we all matter. It doesn't matter that we are different. It takes all kinds to make the world go round. That's also true with family. I love and appreciate my family more than I ever have. We are family, and I now thank God for each of them, even the crazy ones, lol. We've started an annual family cookout. The first one had over sixty-five people in attendance who came from near and far. God has blessed us, and I'm forever grateful.

Resurrected Life Christian Outreach Ministry: I have been blessed to be the first person to go through this ministry. My life is what God used to establish it. Resurrected life is a ministry that God placed in me a long time ago. However, it hadn't been proven to work. I am positive proof that it does. God can and will resurrect any and every life if we give Him the chance. There will be different branches of this ministry, such as:

Companions will be a ministry that deals with the seniors in our community. We will make sure they have basic needs and are able to interact with each other in a safe environment. We will offer outings for them free of charge based on what they want to do. We want them to know they are not forgotten.

Resurrected Life is a homeless shelter that will be divided into three divisions for singles, married couples, and families. There will be different programs available to fit the needs of each person or family.

Transitions is a home designed to reintroduce residents back into society after being incarcerated. All residents must be court-ordered.

Food and Clothing Pantry, which will be open to anyone in need. This will be done through donations.

I Am My Sister's Keeper is a ministry designed to disciple women of all ages through the Word and personal experiences. (active)

I Am My Brother's Keeper is a ministry designed to disciple men of all ages through the Word of God and personal experiences. (active)

Resurrected Life3: Table Talk Podcast is a ministry that teaches the Word of God through ordinary conversation that the listeners get to overhear. It is found on Spotify.

The Land of Goshen is a ministry that will transport its clients back and forth to doctors' appointments, grocery stores, family outings, etc. It is geared to those vulnerable adults whose regular modes of transportation do not work. Private pay and insurance are accepted. All donations will go back into the ministry! We will also provide utility assistance as funds are available.

These ministries will be free of charge to the recipients. Therefore, the goal is to use business and, eventually, donations to support the ministry. I am also donating 10% of my book sales to help in this effort. Additionally, we host the Resurrected Life Morning Bible Study (FB Live) to provide spiritual nourishment and guidance. We have a long way to go before all these ministries manifest, but with God, all things are possible one step at a time!

These were just some of the things that God promised and have done so far in my life. He is no respecter of a person; therefore, whatever He has spoken over your life shall come to pass if you trust and believe him. Remember Mark 11:24, Therefore I say unto you, all things, whatsoever you ask when ye pray, believe that you shall receive; and they shall come unto you. God will do what He said.

My Prayer for You: Dear God, I pray this prayer on behalf of the person reading this book. I declare and decree that whether they be saved or unsaved, God, breathe upon them and their situation. God, I ask that you open their hearts to hear and receive your Word through this book. Lord, I ask that they develop a relationship with you that is like none other. That it becomes unique and not a carbon copy of what their mother or father had. Show yourself strong in their lives so that they can no longer deny the power of the sacrifice you made that day on the cross. God, I also declare that they will shut the door of the devil by denying themselves and trusting and depending on You, God. Oh God, you did it for me; now God do it for them. I believe this book can and will change lives. Do it God in them and in me. Whatever your will is, I declare and decree that it shall be done. I thank you in advance; in Jesus' Name, Amen!

In conclusion, this journey was not easy, but it was necessary. It doesn't matter what you've done or how long you have been doing it. God will receive you if you only ask.

Prayer of Salvation: God, I ask you to come into my heart right now. I have forsaken your way, and I'm sorry. I know that I can't live this life without you, and I'm tired of trying. I believe in the death, burial, and resurrection of Jesus. He is the one who died for me. I confess with my mouth, and I believe in my heart that you are my Lord and Savior. In Jesus' name, I pray, Amen!

I pray that you, too, find your way into God's purpose. God loves you, and I do, too. Hold on and keep the faith, and I promise it will sustain you. God bless. By the way, guess who's getting married?

ABOUT THE AUTHOR

Robin Annette Wages was born on August 27, 1969, in Columbia, SC, and currently resides in Conway, SC, where she relocated to pursue ministry work. Embracing the fivefold ministry as Apostle, Pastor, Evangelist, Prophet, and Teacher, she leads her outreach efforts. In addition to her spiritual roles, she cherishes her roles as a daughter, mother, sister, aunt, cousin, and soon-to-be wife. She is licensed and ordained in non-denominational ministry, founding Resurrected Life Christian Outreach Ministry. She is also licensed and ordained by the Kingston Lake Baptist Association, serving her local Assembly.

Currently pursuing a Bachelor's degree in Christian Ministry at Mid-America Christian University, she is six classes away from certification as a Pastor and Christian Counselor. Her commitment extends beyond academia; she is actively engaged in community service, offering prayer, distributing food, cooking in community kitchens, providing indigent bags, and offering support to those facing challenges. Her journey has led her to a place of freedom, enabling her to fulfill her purpose of serving God and His people wholeheartedly.

Made in the USA
Columbia, SC
23 October 2024

44505821R00167